FIELDING PRACTICE: A Study of the Novels of Henry Fielding

The illustrations in this volume are taken from two early Dutch translations of Fielding. Three come from *Historie van den Vondeling Thomas Jones,* uit het Engelsch vertaald door P. le Clercq, Amsterdam 1749: the one on the front cover which shows Tom Jones saving Mrs Waters from her assailant Northerton; that on p. 33 which is of Blifil entering Mr Allworthy's presence for his unmasking, and that on p. 135 of Black George persuading Sophia to eat some of the chicken he has served her, and which turns out to contain a letter from Tom.

The other two are from *De Historie of Gevallen van Joseph Andriessen,* na den laatste druk uit 't Engels vertaelt, Amsterdam 1776: the one on p. 61, showing the ducking-joke played on Parson Adams, and the one at the end, of the procession to the church in the final chapter of the novel.

NEW SERIES VOLUME 44

COSTERUS

Rodopi

Amsterdam 1984

FIELDING PRACTICE

A Study of the Novels of Henry Fielding

by

JOHN JAMES PEEREBOOM

CIP-GEGEVENS

Peereboom, John James

Fielding practice: A study of the novels of Henry
Fielding / John James Peereboom. — Amsterdam : Rodopi. —
(Costerus ; vol. 44)
Met lit. opg.
ISBN 90-6203-955-3
SISO enge 853.6 UDC 820"17"
Trefw. : Fielding, Henri / Engelse letterkunde : 18e eeuw.
©Editions Rodopi B.V., Amsterdam 1984
Printed in the Netherlands

CONTENTS

PREFACE

It is hard to form a convincing estimate of the importance of literature in modern societies. For a number of people it might as well not exist; a smaller number, many of whom help to produce it, live with it day and night. So much is unmistakable, but what is the status of that small number, and what is the influence of their opinions?

Clearly the influence extends beyond the limited circle to include those who take an active interest in literature, who go to lectures and join clubs, or at any rate read review pages and weekly supplements. What do they get out of this? In many cases, they must be looking for more than just distraction, judging by the seriousness and elaborateness of the information they take in. For some of them at least it looks as if literature has come to replace what used to be called the spiritual life. With the decline of organized religion, the handiest means to keep in touch with what is being thought and felt about the human condition may well be literature, together with its fringe of discussions and reviews.

The literary spiritual life does not pretend to give insights of eternal validity. It is tied to the development of the culture it belongs to; or rather, it forms part of that development, and the intellectual and the educated layman have to be, unlike the believers of old, constantly on the move to keep up with new ideas. What they seek is not profundity, and what they want to overcome is not fear of death; they are after variety, and they are afraid of getting bogged down.

If one thinks of modern civilization as mostly concerned to get to the next phase in each of its various lines of development, just being on the move may be the complete answer to our quest. What does it matter what literature contains, as long as it is different, or differently put from what we were used to? No one knows what is important, in a world without recognizable direction into its far from assured future. As long as we are not bored, that is all we can ask.

Yet at the same time criticism still uses quite freely words like important, and revealing, and liberating, and penetrating, and thoughtful, and even profound. It does not confine itself to epithets like exciting and fascinating, that belong to our culture on the move. The hope remains that we may be moving not just desperately forward, but upwards or inwards as well.

Upwards or inwards to what or where it is impossible to say. What is it that literature can offer, apart from newness? The experience of a number of years of writing incidental book reviews, often of foreign books few of which qualified automatically for discussion, is bound to include frequent confrontations with the question. Having enjoyed a novel, one wants to encourage people to read it, but it has always been exceedingly difficult to think of a reason why they should if they had other things to do. One could recommend to them the absorbing story to take them out of their daily routine, if the novel happened to be of that type. In other and sometimes in the same cases, one could insist on the delights provided by the author's use of words and turn of phrases. In any case there was bound to be a stimulus for the imagination, and often for the intelligence as well; and although novels are not the only places where one can find these, they are congenial places for those who likes books. And then there is this liking of books as a consideration in its own right: the pleasure of holding the object and turning its leaves, the reduction of the world to a size that can be apprehended by the imagination, and the isolation of the reader from his surroundings.

All these are sound arguments for doing some reading occasionally, but they apply to so many books that they can provide no critical standards, nor can they hold out a prospect of a share in such spiritual life as we have left. We would need more: an understanding of the human condition, and perhaps of what we could do with it; something at any rate beyond mere enjoyment of the description of imaginary people's lives.

As far as the eye can reach, no reviewer or critic or other expert tells us where to find the secret of literary importance. What can prospective readers expect to know or understand or have experienced, after finishing a given book, that they lacked before? All they are in the habit of being enlightened about is whether the book deserves to be called good or an equivalent adjective, as well of course as fascinating or exciting. 'Good' has been reduced to a miserable term of recommendation. Whether used by the literary expert who assumes an expression of remote contempt for those who will fail to see its justice, or pronounced with eagerness by people who do not claim to know what they are talking about, one's heart sinks whenever one hears that something is good. Good in what sense, and for what, and for whom, and how do you know?

Dissatisfaction not just with that one word, but with the possibilities of qualification in general can be regarded as the dominant mood behind the following attempt to find terms for judging Fielding. It might be argued that a contemporary writer would have made a better subject for this exercise than one from the past, who has a right to more critical circumspection. From time to time, it is useful to remind oneself of what T.S. Eliot pronounced in reply to those who might feel that 'we *know* so much more' than the classics: 'Precisely; and they are that which we know.'[1]

There is doubtless truth in this, and we must assume in the case of Fieldings as of others that some of his insights have been absorbed into our collective consciousness or our millions of private consciousnesses; that we know some things because he formulated them, and it would ill become us to run him down for banality two hundred years later. At the same time it has to be pointed out that the classics of European literature have not been absorbed by any reader's consciousness to the extent of losing their individual identity. Many of them open our eyes more frequently and decisively than most works by contemporaries, and they do so in a variety of ways. If their position in the history of literature depended on what they had given away to our consciousness, we would find only the remains of their great days in them, and have to think ourselves back into the past to discover their original shape; but the point is that we have not finished with them yet.

Another reservation is that if we take Eliot's view entirely seriously it can lead to an unspoken assumption that the author's contemporaries shared a pattern of life and experience, which made 'them' react in a way that 'we' no longer will. 'We' should then be supposed to have our own response in common, again

1. T.S. Eliot, 'Tradition and the Individual Talent,' *Selected Essays,* p.6.

determined by our place in history. It seems a fallacy. If there is one thing a familiarity with reviewing suggests it is that agreement between contemporaries is rarely more than skin-deep; and it is a common experience to feel surprise or dismay at what some experts call a masterpiece, as it is to have one's imagination fired by a novel nobody appears to have noticed. 'Literary history often stresses the individuality of a period without placing a correspondent stress on discordant individualities within a period'.[2]

It seems justifiable to judge Fielding on one's own terms even after more than two hundred years, taking into account as much as one knows and understands of the eighteenth century, and without trying to force from him answers to questions that later times have raised. The attempt is not to see him as a representative of his century and as a human period piece; nor is it to dress him up in modern costume and pretend he is one of us. His voice is distant, and we have to listen carefully, but it is not beyond us to determine directly what significance should be attached to his writing in various veins.

The attempt to appreciate Fielding in a spirit of scepticism about literary values and classical status has one inevitable consequence which is that his voice will gradually begin to sound smaller than it used to. Normally, the trappings of classical status have an amplifying effect. Even when we are bored by an author with an assured place in the history of literature, we cannot help being impressed. It is no mean achievement to survive oneself in writing. Words that have gone through dozens of editions will not lightly be dismissed as pointless even when that is what they seem to be.

Added to the passing of the time, there is the 'critical heritage': the ideas of all those who have analysed and judged the works of the masters. For readers who have no intention of concerning themselves with critical studies, the very thought that eminent people have considered it worth becoming authorities on an *oeuvre* gives further power to its voice. For readers who do consult them the critics, being personalities in their own right engaged in debate with each other, may well demand so much attention that little is left for the master himself. In that case they cannot be said to amplify the original voice, but they do create a sense of literary

2. E.D. Hirsch, Jr., *The Aims of Interpretation,* p.38.

occasion, with all their new voices surrounding the original one.

By comparison, the original voice seems a modest one; even Fielding's, noisy though he could be. He was a moralist of course, firm with his contemporaries on a variety of questions of conduct; but how much significance do his views possess either for his own novels or for the world outside? He was a comic writer unmistakably, but Swift and Sterne were funnier, and how often can we be said to remember him for the laughter he has caused? He had a strongly developed sense of literary form, and could construct a novel like an architect; but although this allows us to make graphs showing how everything fits together, it is a doubtful contribution to our reading pleasure or our insight into human affairs.

The first three chapters that follow deal with these constituent elements of Fieldings's talent, and provide an estimate of their share in the enduring value of the novels. They confirm that much of his strength lies in his views on conduct, in his comedy and in his constructions; certainly more than in for instance his psychology, or his descriptions or his profundity. At the same time it looks as if the yield of these objective qualities is more variable than it is usually said to be, and between them they do not account for the continuing vividness of Fielding's image among us. The fourth chapter attempts to balance them by clarifying the picture of his own personality that emerges from his work, and by arguing that it is the perception of his reality rather than of his fictions that keeps us interested in him.

On the way to this conclusion a certain amount of depreciation of passages and aspects of the novels under discussion occurs which might make the reader suspect a desire to relegate them to a lower order of classics. Chapter V intends to correct this impression. Excellence in anyone and in anyone's work is an intermittent thing. Our best moments happen infrequently; such is the human condition, from which Fielding was no more exempt than are other authors. Much of his writing, although it may help to make the stories and the arguments cohere, is of no value in itself. It deserves the same patience and consideration we show when we have to listen to our friends and neighbours and ourselves talking on an ordinary day, with no more than average perception or inventiveness; if we feel obliged to admire it, we only cause confusion and spoil our taste for better things. The main purpose of Chapter V is to make clear that Fielding did not stand alone in this respect. It puts him in perspective.

As a result of all this his figure should look a little sparer than before, but not to his disadvantage; more recognizably a figure on a human scale, even if immortal.

I THE MORALIST

i

The days when Henry Fielding had a bad name are behind us. There used to be many critics and biographers who thought he had probably led a dissolute life, and that in any case his casualness when he tolds us of Tom Jones being paid by Lady Bellaston for services in bed showed there was something wrong with his moral standards. Not that there was ever a firm consensus. Dr. Johnson's pronouncement on Fielding: 'What I mean by his being a block-head is that he was a barren rascal',[1] puzzled Boswell and has puzzled others. Without being quite a barren rascal, however, Fielding could still be dubious. Coleridge who admired him thought an additional paragraph in the Lady Bellaston story 'would have removed in great measure any just objections — at all events relatively to Fielding himself, and with regard to the state of manners at the time.'[2]

The feeling that Tom Jones needed more apologies was widely shared in the nineteenth century, and memorably expressed by Thackeray ('... that odious broad-backed Mr Jones carries off his beauty with scarce an interval of remorse for his many errors and shortcomings ...'),[3] although taken as a whole his critical appraisal struck Wilbur Cross, and may still strike us after another sixty years, as 'the most eloquent tribute that has ever been paid to the genius and character of Fielding.'[4] As a novelist Fielding has normally had recognition if not always admiration through the

1. Boswell's *Life of Johnson* (O.U.P. edition, Oxford/London 1953), p. 480.
2. A note, in *Miscellaneous Criticism* (ed. T.M. Rayner), quoted in Claude Rawson (ed.), *Henry Fielding, a Critical Anthology,* p. 206.
3. W.M. Thackeray, *The English Humourists of the Eighteenth Century,* p. 584.
4. Wilbur L. Cross, *The History of Henry Fielding,* Vol. III, p. 216. Cross's remains the standard biography of Fielding.

years since 1754; as a private person and a moralist, he was discussed with varying degrees of disapproval.

This is so no longer. We have shaken off what Cross called 'the incubus of Arthur Murphy.'[5] Murphy, when he published the first collected works of Fielding in 1762, wrote a biographical essay as an introduction, and being short of facts supplied a large number of anecdotes, many of which were damaging, and although he was forgivingly disposed others were not.[6] All through Victorian times a slightly disreputable air continued to cling to Fielding. Fortunately for his memory we are less suspicious as well as less strict. There is nothing he particularly needs to be condemned for in the limited number of facts that we know; and if there were something we would be less inclined to bother about it than our grandfathers.

What we do know of him allows us to pronounce him one of the few English novelists who must have been a good and friendly man. His good temper and his zest for life, the mildness of his agression in an age when literary men went out of their way to be vicious, his devotion to his first wife and his attachment to the second, his industry and honesty as a magistrate in Bow Street, his scepticism about human excellence and his delight in it: all this, and a wealth of detail that points the same way, clearly raise him above the strictures inspired by Murphy. Nor did he stop at himself. He wanted other people to be good too, and one of the aims of his books was to tell them what he meant by that. To the modern reader this is usually so obvious that far from thinking him a barren rascal, we are in danger of regarding him as primarily a literary preacher. Martin Battestin has warned us against such a view in his book on the moral content of *Joseph Andrews*. He is prepared to concede that Fielding is 'fundamentally a moralist,' but he thinks it worth pointing out that what is 'most memorable' about him 'is not his morality or his religion, but his comedy — the warm breath of laughter that animates his fiction.'[7]

We should not exaggerate, but even in the days when we were inclined to frown over what we thought were Fielding's faults, we could not have failed to notice his moral concern. 'I describe not

5. ibid., III, p. 249.

6. Arthur Murphy, *The Works of Henry Fielding, Esq.,* 4 Vols. London, 1762.

7. Martin C. Battestin, *The Moral Basis of Fieldings's Art,* p. x.

men, but manners; not an individual, but a species,' he wrote in the introductory chapter to Book III of *Joseph Andrews,* and he went on to explain that his picture of a lawyer in an earlier chapter was not intended 'to expose one pitiful wretch to the small and contemptible circle of his acquaintance; but to hold the glass to thousand in their closets, that they may contemplate their deformity, and endeavour to reduce it, and thus by suffering private mortification may avoid public shame' (*Joseph Andrews,* p.216).

Such was his purpose. Would he be mortified if he were allowed to return to life and see how little improvement his words had brought about? The legal profession rarely comes in for the amount of criticism that this eighteenth-century learned friend levelled at them; but as a whole the world has not definably improved. It is not certain that Fielding would be upset. When he described the sailors jeering at him as he was carried aboard the ship that was to take him to Lisbon and his death in 1754, he called it 'a lively picture of that cruelty and inhumanity in the nature of men which I have often contemplated with concern and which leads the mind into a train of very uncomfortable and melancholy thoughts' (*Journal of a Voyage to Lisbon,* pp. 200-1).

That was a different time of Fielding's life, which could easily produce different views. It is true, though, that he had contemplated our inhumanity 'with concern' on many earlier occasions. Jonathan Wild and Blifil, Trulliber and Trent, Shamela and Mrs Bennet's stepmother are all capable of inspiring melancholy thoughts; and nowhere in Fielding's work do we have to search very long for further examples. So many of his creations show unpleasant and vicious traits that it is surprising to find him cheerful and full of comedy much of the time. Knowing humanity as we do we are not easily baffled by contradictions and apparent incompatibilities, but it would be a pity if we lost all feeling for the strangeness of them. It is the most obvious strangeness of Fielding that he should combine his black view of human conduct with his relaxed notion of good nature and the eager freshness typical of his style. It is one of the less strange things about him that his vision should have clouded over and become less colourful by the time he wrote *Amelia.*

Fielding as a moralist is not a subject that lends itself easily to proper definition. What did he think he was doing, and how much does it mean for us? One could adopt the view that he did not amount to much as a moralist, which is what F.R. Leavis said who disliked him so much that he thought him important mostly 'because he leads to Jane Austen, to appreciate whose distinction is to feel that life isn't long enough to permit of one's giving much time to Fielding.'[8] Certainly one has never heard of readers trying to revivify their moral sense by confrontations with Adams and Amelia. They go to Fielding for the story and the laughs, and sometimes for the author's style of presentation, which makes one think of a modern nobleman showing the crowd round his stately home and finding himself enjoying it. With such expectations, they are inevitably disappointed by *Amelia;* but *Joseph Andrews* and *Tom Jones* still satisfy.

An attempt to provide a further estimate of Fielding's worth as a novelist could not be carried out by defining the origin and content of his concept of good nature and his rules of conduct. For one thing all this has been done by Professor Battestin;[9] for another, an author's views on morality have no direct bearing on the quality of his novels. We do not read novels in order to remedy any vagueness we may suffer from about how to behave in our own lives; nor to find confirmation of long-held views. What the novelist and the moralist can do for us is to show moral principles in conflict with other motives, and to bring that conflict to life so that we recognize it as related to our own. Beyond that, the novel can suggest how the author has come to terms, and not necessarily friendly terms, with these problems of man's condition.

It is no use telling us what to do and how to behave. Novel-reading has nothing to do with New Year resolutions. What we should be able to discover when we find the moralist in the novelist is the experience of moral doubt, ambition and dissatisfaction. Its presence does not automatically elevate the novelist, nor its absence condemn him. It is a matter of definition of content.

ii

In a search for the experience of moral conflict we are bound to be disappointed if we look inside Fielding's characters. His concern was almost exclusively with the external manifestations of human-

8. F.R. Leavis, *The Great Tradition,* p. 159.
9. Battestin, *The Moral Basis of Fielding's Art,* p. 11.

ity; the inner world was Richardson's territory. This does not mean that moral experience could only be straightforward in Fielding. There is ample scope for conflict in the author's own relationship with his characters; and if all were straightforward there, we should not have the difficulty that we do in making up our minds about what they stand for.

There are critics, for instance, who take the character of Joseph Andrews seriously. Maurice Johnson, quoting as an influence on him a critic who has argued that Joseph becomes a true hero after Book II ch. xii, saw enough truth in him even in that chapter to write that in contrast with the conventional terms of the song Fanny hears him sing 'the deep-felt love of Joseph and Fanny seems like a brilliant moment out of life itself.'[10] More soberly J. Paul Hunter, in a chapter whose main argument is that Fielding at first persuades his reader to laugh at Joseph's morality and then surprises him by taking it seriously, says that 'Once Fielding delivers Joseph from his bondage to foolishness and allows him to grow into a mature, sensible hero, such readers are left holding their own gullibility.'[11]

A mature, sensible hero? It is a difficult description to accept, reluctant as we may be to look down on such a harmless paragon. All critics tend to agree that he is meant to make us laugh in the early chapters, where not only his employer and her 'waiting-gentlewoman' but the very birds in the trees are said to have found him irresistible (*Joseph Andrews*, p. 27). For such an enchanter to be too naive to see what Lady Booby is talking about when she tries to lure him into her bed is generally thought funny. A mature, sensible hero would not have that problem.

In those chapters, therefore, when we laugh we can be fairly sure that Fielding would have enjoyed the sound. Later on, a little before the middle of the novel, he may have hoped we would change the tune of our response. Male chastity is not necessarily a funny thing, and Fielding was certainly not writing in praise of libertinism. Also, Joseph added to his negative virtue the positive one of his love for Fanny. When 'This modest creature, whom no warmth in summer could ever induce to expose her charms to the

10. Maurice Johnson, *Fielding's Art of Fiction,* pp. 54-5. The critic he quotes is Dick Taylor, Jr.

11. J. Paul Hunter, *Occasional Form,* p. 104.

wanton sun,' loses her handkerchief and suffers great discomfort from Joseph's staring at her bosom, he realizes this and looks away. 'So great was his fear of offending her, and so truly did his passion for her deserve the noble name of love' (*Joseph Andrews,* p. 347). Perhaps one could take this with absolute seriousness; but one could also suspect a touch of parody. Fielding must have been conscious of a measure of overstatement when he brought in the 'noble name of love' about a chaste young man who turns his eyes away from his girl's breasts because he notices her embarrassment.

If one refuses to accept Joseph's sensible maturity this need not be because one thinks Fielding is still mocking him — although it is fair to say that he makes it difficult for us to take everything he says literally in, for instance, the battle with the hounds (*Joseph Andrews,* pp. 271-3). The argument would rather be that having started as a comic outline Joseph never fills up with enough flesh and blood to force a reversal of our judgment. He is simply a young man in love who is not to be tempted by strange ladies and who is prepared to lay about him with a stick when the occasion demands. Although there is nothing wrong with him, he is a figure of slight importance.

Without going into the question of how much of this novel is a retort to *Pamela,* one may say that surely it all began with the figure of Joseph intended to exemplify a higher moral standard than Richardson's heroine. As it turned out, he did not get very far. His chastity was more heroic than his supposed sister's because unlike her he had to brave his readers' laughter; and his fidelity in love was more commendable than hers because Fanny unlike Mr B. had no status and financial security to offer. Beyond that, the idea of Joseph is not associated with any merit or struggle or conflict to speak of.

If one assumes that Fielding thought more or less the same thing about him, the course of *Joseph Andrews* right up to the end seems more rapidly acceptable and explicable than if one tries to give him his full human weight. Opposing a more substantial morality to Pamela's not convincingly disinterested protection of her virtue demanded more than a pretty young man. It demanded Parson Adams, who did not have his eye on any juicy awards, did not work himself up over the idea of his own virtue, and was not designed as an example of flawless purity.

One of the great things about Adams, perhaps not always sufficiently stressed, is that apart from not being pure and beautiful he is also a bore. Not that he bores us as readers. He would bore us if we were in the novel with him, or if he should step out of it. His main weakness as a social companion is his tendency to talk interminably about his own concerns, such as Homer or the latitudinarian divines, and be in the dark about what goes on in the world beyond his limited circle. It is a perfectly tolerable defect to read about, but it does mean that we have to imagine him as a tiresome companion.

This should not be taken for a licence to detract from Adam's virtues. He has two principal ones: no power or influence can shift him when his religious conviction is involved, and he is fearless when it comes to defending women and friends against bullies. Whether his innocence should count as a third virtue may be a fit matter for dispute. Although a clergyman at the age of fifty or more may have the right to be as unworldly as he is, one imagines his parishioners might wonder if they would not be better off with a curate who noticed things.[12] Fielding has an excellent time making him react explosively to various details in Mr Wilson's lengthy story of his sinful past.

> She was indeed a coquette achevée. 'Pray, sir,' says Adams, 'what is a coquette? I have met with the word in French authors, but never could assign any idea to it. I believe it is the same with *une sotte*, Anglicè, *a fool*.' 'Sir,' answered the gentleman, 'perhaps you are not much mistaken.'

For a schoolmaster and father of eleven Adams is a little silly though, however understanding Mr Wilson may be; and his exclamation of 'Good Lord! what wicked times are these!' seems unworthy of a man as well-read as he is (*Joseph Andrews*, pp. 237 and 230).

And what of his vanity? 'Indeed, if this good man had an enthusiasm, or what the vulgar call a blind side, it was this: he thought a schoolmaster the greatest character in the world, and himself the greatest of schoolmasters: neither of which points he would have given up to Alexander the Great at the head of his army' (*Joseph Andrews*, p.263). That surely is not an immediately

---

12. On p. 30 of *Joseph Andrews* his age is given as fifty; on p. 59 he is said to have thirty-five years of parish experience.

attractive side of Adams, and although these qualities are presented to us with delight and verve, Fielding cannot have thought that
it was. If he had wanted to show that an old man can be just as
charming as a young one, he would have gone about it differently.
What he is doing here is drawing the Rev. William Young, who
was a friend of his, in heightened colours. The digression on Mrs
Slipslop and her view of 'high people' and 'low people' ends with
the suggestion that all this would make most sense 'if the gods,
according to the opinion of some, made men only to laugh at
them' (*Joseph Andrews*, p. 182). It is said in a different spirit from
anything that would be directly applicable to Adams; but taken
out of its context and set in a rosier light, it fits the treatment
Fielding gives him very nicely.

His moral qualities, his weaknesses and his oddities are all part
of the same argument. Its starting-point is that purity can never be
fully human, whether in Pamela or in Joseph; and the final point is
that what humanity amounts to is roughly hewn lumps of personality like Adams, and that any lifelike representation of
morally responsible conduct has to take into account the hopeless
irregularity of human nature.

A just man is a possibility, but he is bound to look odd and to
have many faults. Whether this was the view Fielding intended to
express, or if it was forced on to him by the course the novel took
as it developed may be an impossible question to answer firmly in
one sense. Trying to interpret the story of Mr Wilson, one might
imagine that he intended something else. Battestin has argued that
Wilson's moral slide is meant to show 'what might have happened
to Joseph Andrews himself had he lacked the good advice and
good example of Parson Adams. With Wilson's adoption of the
classical ideal of life his own pilgrimage is complete, symbolically
reinforcing the movement of the novel as a whole, and a moral
alternative is established in contrast to the ways of vanity.'[13]

In Battestin's view, the Wilson story has a clear point, and a full
share in the meaning of the novel. For others, it is better
understood as a formal exercise. J. Paul Hunter, discussing the
interpolations in general, says that 'These worlds are counter-
worlds, and their laws, characters and tones imitate the ways of
traditions contemporaneous with Fielding but different in method,

13. Battestin, *The Moral Basis of Fielding's Art,* p. 129.

intention or both.'[14] The purpose would be not to give added strength to the moral significance of Joseph but to provide a contrast between conventional old-style narration and the novel's new one. Glenn W. Hatfield offers a similar interpretation, with a stronger emphasis on the parodic intention: 'The effect is achieved by heightening the superlative and minute artifice of the parody, so that what surrounds it, the bulk of the work, seems "real" by comparison.'[15]

These formal interpretations are bound to have an appeal for the present-day reader, who is unlikely to be convinced by the moral significance of stories like that of Mr Wilson. Still, perhaps Battestin's view can be accomodated as well. Fielding may have had hidden intentions occasionally, to confirm this and parody that, but seeing them defined one wonders what was to stop him carrying out several of them at the same time. The argument from tradition, that he put in interpolations just because Cervantes and others had done so, could also be added. Why not have a good old-fashioned image of the simple and true life? It would be perfectly relevant, unlike some other interpolations; and as a further charm it could have a Hogarthian look about it: 'I soon exchanged the bailiff's house for a prison; where, as I had not money sufficient to procure me a separate apartment, I was crowded in with a great number of miserable wretches, in common with whom I was destitute of every convenience of life, even that which all the brutes enjoy, wholesome air' (*Joseph Andrews,* p.249).

Every reader, Fielding may have reflected, should find something to enjoy in such interpolations. A classical foundation and a top of modern parody, and the moral content of the work epitomized in between: no one could wish for more. Perhaps what eighteenth-century readers saw mostly in this form was a tribute to the idea of literature. A similar phenomenon occurs frequently in our own day. Readers do not know what to like, nor do they know what life is about, or to what extent literature should reflect it; but they can recognize certain conventional signs denoting literature. It seems plausible to assume that at least a number of educated

14. Hunter, *Occasional Form,* p. 154.
15. Glenn W. Hatfield, *Henry Fielding and the Language of Irony,* p. 200.

readers of the 1740s accepted Wilson on these terms, and that Fielding hoped that they would.

As a moralist the story makes him look stilted if we assume that he was serious about Wilson. To soften that impression, as we cannot properly get rid of it, the best explanation would be that Fielding was trying out a variety of techniques. He did feel like a cultural mediator between the past and the future, initiating a new genre. He could not be expected to know exactly what he was achieving. He was experimenting in various directions, backwards and forwards. In the circumstances it was up to the reader, whether in the eighteenth or in the twentieth century, to determine if his concept of moral man would go more easily with the smoothness of Wilson or the hairiness of Adams.

The superior validity of Adams has perhaps been determined by the subsequent course of Western civilization. For most readers nowadays man should be more easily recognizable in a roughly hewn lump than in a well-organized soul on its way to judgment. However, if the dictates of civilization were not compelling enough there would still be the development of the novel. Adams could hold his own among characters of Jane Austen or Dickens; Wilson could not. So Adams had time on his side, but it was not as if Fielding had now solved his moral problem, with his eyes trained on the future. In *Tom Jones* it occurs again. Here two of the characters divide the bulk of the moral fibre between them, the hero and Allworthy. This time it is age which represents the purity that Joseph had to incarnate in the earlier novel; the human defects go to Tom.

One could argue for a while about which of the two views of youth versus age is more tenable. In most disputes the conclusion would be that *Joseph Andrews* wins. Purity may always be an illusion, but it looks less silly at twenty than at fifty. It is therefore not surprising that Fielding fails with his quinquagenarian. This is not because it is impossible to imagine somebody like Allworthy. There is no known limit to the variety of human individuals that reality can contain, and far more unlikely characters have been recorded. Mere viability, however, is not enough. For a plausible character in a novel like this, without any descriptions of inner experience, the further requirement is that we respond to his creator's view of him.

It is widely recognized that this is too much to ask in the case of

Allworthy. His self-satisfied misjudgments are too glaring for a landowner of even moderate wisdom. E. Taiwo Palmer has made a brave attempt to save him as a character, using Empson's discovery of double irony to argue that Fieldings shows him up while appearing to praise him.[16] Although this was ingenious and at least partially convincing, Allworthy remains unable to live up to his nominal reputation. Something is saved when Fielding tells us that we should not blame Allworthy for his inability to see Thwackum's unpleasant side as clearly as we do, from our privileged vantage point (*Tom Jones,* I, p. 125). Still, even if we appreciate that point the objection against this good man remains. He might be unable to see the things we see; but he should have developed more scepticism in the face of stories told him by obviously unreliable people about his friends and protégés.

Even after reading about Allworthy we may be able to believe that it is possible for landowners of great wealth, who in some traits resemble Fielding's benefactor Ralph Allen,[17] to be men of excellent morality; but we have not received any new evidence for our belief. We cannot, on the other hand, put Allworthy on a footing with Wilson and Joseph Andrews as an artificial element in the novel, acceptable if viewed as such. Allworthy is not artificial; he is a false natural.

To call Tom Jones himself a real natural would be to mistake Fielding's treatment of him; but he goes far enough in the direction of naturalness to give us some of the excitement of discovering a human being. It is true that he starts out as unmistakably Fielding's no less than Allworthy's blue-eyed boy. He will show us that *good nature* really exists, and give us confidence that the mean and the wicked who infest too much of the world will never have it all their own way. Tom is not the type who has learned by heart what to say in order to create an impression of moral soundness, like his bigoted foster-brother Blifil. He tends to say the wrong things; but he feels the right ones, an experience unknown to Blifil. Tom is warm-hearted and generous and courageous and honest; he

16. E.Taiwo Palmer, 'Irony in *Tom Jones*,' *MLR*, XVI (1971), 497-510.

17. Allen was praised, although not quite named, in Fielding's Dedication in *Tom Jones*; see Cross, *The History of Henry Fielding*, II, p. 162.

is insensitive to philosophical cant and to religious cant; he is never tired, and he looks splendid.

Nor is this all. If it were, he would be simply too good to be true. Fortunately he has faults, and not in the same sense as Parson Adams who can be tiresome in company but never does anything that he knows to be morally reprehensible. Tom actually commits faults. He does not go very far; nothing criminal, nothing cowardly or mean or ungenerous can be imputed to him. Still, he does go to bed with Lady Bellaston, in spite of being constantly in love with Sophia; and he accepts money from her, which makes this relationship stand out as more reprehensible than his adventures with Molly and Mrs Waters.

Tom is far from being unrestrictedly permissive, as he makes clear when he indicts Nightingale's treatment of Nancy Miller.

> 'Lookee, Mr Nightingale,' said Jones, 'I am no canting hypocrite, nor do I pretend to the gift of chastity, more than my neighbours. I have been guilty with women, I own it; but I am not conscious that I have ever injured any — nor would I to procure pleasure to myself, be knowingly the cause of misery to any human being' (*Tom Jones,* III, p. 108).

Tom knows how far he can go and still have Fielding's support, even if not Dr Johnson's or Thackeray's. It must be admitted that none of his three love affairs had any element of seduction of the innocent in it. He would never have tried such liberties with Sophia, we are to assume — not that she would have given him much of a chance.

We need not blame Tom Jones very hard, and in fact there are readers to whom it has never occurred to do so. A question worth considering is whether these sexual liberties are not precisely what saves Tom as a human being. Without them, he would be too unrelievedly and blandly delightful. That *good nature* of his is heartening as far as it goes, but without any evidence of inner struggle and precariousness of victory it loses touch with life outside the book if we have nothing to set against it. Worse than that, it drifts out of touch with Fielding's own sense of real human beings; or so at any rate it looks for instance in the dialogue in Book XIV where Jones is asking Nightingale how he can get rid of Lady Bellaston. He explains why it is not easy: " 'No, my friend, but I am under obligations to her, and very great ones. Since you know so much, I will be very explicit with you. It is owing perhaps solely to her, that I have not, before this, wanted a bit of bread. How can I possibly desert such a woman?' " Nightingale asks him if the woman for whom Lady Bellaston must be deserted is a case of 'an honourable mistress'. " 'Honourable?' answered Jones; 'no breath ever yet durst sully her reputation. The sweetest air is not purer, the limpid stream not clearer than her honour. She is all over, both in mind and body, consummate perfection' " (*Tom Jones*, III, pp. 181-2).

Even if one takes this eulogy to be partly an exercise in language and partly an homage to the memory of Charlotte Cradock, Fielding's first wife on whom as he says he had modelled Sophia (III, p. 30), it is obvious that the novel lives in what Jones says about the awkward situation and not in the expression of his great love. It would be irresponsible to suggest that Fielding was getting bored with the goodness of the Tom-and-Sophia relationship. What can be seen here without excessive imaginative licence is another example of the novel demanding its tribute of realism. The faults of Tom Jones function like the defects of Abraham Adams: they preserve these characters from inhuman purity, and make them live.

One could argue that viewed in this light there is more life in Adams than in Jones, his defects being incurable, unlike the young man's peccadilloes. There may be something in this, but as an observation on its own it does not carry much weight. Novel characters do not function independently; they acquire their meaning together with the others, and having said something about the good ones of *Joseph Andrews* and *Tom Jones* it is time to look at the black side. There is little to be gained at this stage by lining up the good ones from *Jonathan Wild* and *Amelia* as well. The interest of those books lies elsewhere than in the goodness of the Heartfrees and the Booths, because although they deserve Fielding's praise for their exemplary love-lives they are not morally significant in their stories. They are so much the opposite, passively receiving the blows life deals them and hoping for the best, that they illustrate Fielding's train of melancholy thoughts rather than his moral energy. In the early part of *Amelia* Booth has a relationship in prison with Miss Matthews not unlike that of Tom and Lady Bellaston, even in the matter of financial support; but he has not caused much indignation. There is not enough life in Booth for us to criticize him, we are just sorry for him.

iii

In each of Fielding's novels a battle is being fought between light and darkness, in moral terms, and the main protagonists are always easily identifiable. Not that the wicked, the mean and the unpleasant who incarnate the principle of darkness regularly fight in the same formation. The way they manifest themselves varies more than with the people of the light on the other side. In *Jonathan Wild* they are dominated by the great man, the master of crime himself. In *Joseph Andrews* they seem to be everywhere, operating without leadership or plan, following the instructions of their own deplorable natures. In *Tom Jones* their activities are partially centralized. Blifil is not in command like Wild, but he is the leading figure on the dark side, and although there are several other objectionable characters about, they are not omni-present on Tom Jones's travels as they are on Joseph's. In *Amelia* it is different again, for although the presence of darkness is more pervasive than in the earlier books the evil characters such as we knew them have largely gone, and are replaced by ambiguous ones who often sound dishonest but sometimes undeservedly.

Through the four novels we can say that goodness varies occasionally in its incarnations, from pure to lifelike and from combative to defenceless, but that it remains basically the same. All the good people are in love with their marriage partners, or prospective partners, or at least make excellent husbands, like Adams; they are honest and generous and loyal and cheerful, and they are naive and tend to be cornered by their opponents.

Having observed that the bad vary more in the course of the four novels we can go further and suggest that there is a development in Fielding's views on the subject which means that the similarity between Heartfree and Booth could never have been duplicated between Wild and Amelia's noble lord, or between Didapper and Colonel James. What that development amounts to is that instead of the bad we now have badness as a diffuse element plaguing society. It might be seen as inconsistent that the same process does not occur among the good, and that Booth and Amelia remain mostly in the spotless tradition. In any case it is difficult when one is used to the plain contrast of light and darkness in the worlds of Andrews and Jones, to adapt oneself to the battle of light and twilight in that of the Booths.

At the same time a strong case can be made out for twilight in preference to characters like Jonathan Wild. One can even refuse to see that wholehearted criminal as the hero of a novel, and prefer to call the book a satire on ruthless ambition. Wild, in spite of the historical original behind him, has too little varied substance to count as a lifelike portrait. He is as pure in his villainy as Joseph Andrews in his love.

> 'What have I done then? Why, I have ruined a family, and brought an innocent man to the gallows. I ought rather to weep with Alexander that I have ruined no more, than to regret the little I have done' (*Jonathan Wild,* p. 159).

Fielding would surely have admitted that his purpose could be defined more justly as vexing the world by indicting the mechanism which makes the lazy and the good submit to the wicked and the ruthless than as telling us how it might feel to be a criminal. In the last chapter, the fifteen maxims laid down by Wild for himself, including the one which claims that 'the heart was the proper seat of hatred,' ensures that we shall think of him as a demon rather than a human being (*Jonathan Wild,* p. 203). Still, this is a work of fiction like the three uncontested novels, and in its themes of love and goodness and innocence, and its breezy narration, it resembles them so much that it would be a waste of good examples to leave it out of the discussion on formal grounds.

By comparison with the story of Wild, *Joseph Andrews* is an account of a normally wicked world, full of little people with false pretences. The passengers of the stagecoach in I, xii represent hardly an exaggeration as a cross-section of Fielding's world at this time: they are uniformly mean and indifferent to suffering, and would have been happy to leave Joseph to his injuries and his nakedness by the wayside if the lawyer among them had not pointed out the legal consequences (*Joseph Andrews,* pp. 63-4). Joseph and Adams and Fanny encounter human inadequacy wherever they go, in Tow-wouse and Barnabas, in Pounce and Scout, in Trulliber and Didapper. For a few moments they believe in the comfortable pipe-smoker who sits outside an inn and promises Adams generous help, in II, xvi. It turns out that he is in the habit of not fulfilling his promises, and has done a great deal of harm with them; and to round off our disillusionment at the end of Book II, after the inn-keeper has explained all this to them and has begun to look like one of the few people who sincerely deplore the wickedness of the world, Adams quarrels with him as well (*Joseph Andrews,* pp. 205-211).

Life looks more hopeful when the travellers are refreshed by Mr Wilson's story of redemption and pastoral happiness, but not for long. Soon we find them involved with the squire who invites them to his house after the battle with the hounds. This host and his entourage, all of them nameless and with considerable wealth to back up their taste for violent humour, look more menacing than any other group in the book. When they subject Adams to the laboriously prepared joke of the ducking-stool, one could not have blamed him if he had given in to momentary despair, instead of being merely angry.

Despair was not what Fielding wanted. He hoped he was helping to improve the world, as he explains in the opening chapter of Book III, where he says that he tries to make people look at themselves in order 'that they may contemplate their deformity, and endeavour to reduce it' (see above, page 3). Contemplating their deformity then is what we should expect women to do if they recognize in themselves a resemblance to Mrs Slipslop, Lady Booby's companion, whose lusting after Joseph is even more ridiculous than her employer's because she looks so odd,

> being very short, and rather too corpulent in body, and somewhat red, with the addition of pimples in the face. Her nose was likewise too large, and her eyes too little; nor did she resemble a cow so much in her breath, as in two brown globes which she carried before her; one of her legs was also a little shorter than the other, which occasioned her to limp as she walked (*Joseph Andrews,* p. 40).

Slipslop deserves our pity. An ill-favoured woman, and contemplating her deformity would not help her to get over the brown globes and the limp; or more fairly in accordance with what Fielding says, it will not help any unattractive real women of forty-five who long for male companionship. They will not stop longing, nor find a better technique to force a response out of their reluctant acquaintances. Slipslop as a means to promote good sense and better morals among middle-aged women-servants does not look effective. Trying to say why, one does not even have to put forward the difficulty most people have in controlling either their physical appearance or their sexual urge. It is enough to realize that not a woman alive would recognize herself in Slipslop's hideous image.

There is a difference in kind between the condemnation of Slipslop, who is merely ridiculous, and Trulliber and Pounce and the squires and the lawyers, who do wrong. Does this mean that guilty squires and lawyers would be more ready to recognize themselves? The opposite must be true, in the eighteenth century as in the twentieth. All the impersonal caricatures are easy to get away from, except for readers who are firmly resolved to find a stick to beat themselves with.

In this respect one may be fairly sure that Fielding's influence has been negligible. The wicked and the morally unconcerned have remained as active as they ever were, undismayed by these immortal novels. Never mind, we could say, it was only literature anyway, and the ambition to shock the thousands in their closets was part of the game. There may be something in this, but it is not the last word on the subject. We do not on the whole live with the idea that what novels say about goodness and badness is ipso facto irrelevant; and it does not look as if Fielding thought so. Some of us would probably be content to think that the point of the exercise was only to encourage the good and keep the bad in their places; there is reason to think that that would not have done for Fielding either. He went on writing as if he thought he could change the world, and tried another way in *Tom Jones* where the bad are presented differently again. There is a new type of leading figure in their ranks, in the shape of Blifil. With sanctimoniousness and calculation he brings all the key figures in the Allworthy household on his side, and for a long time he seems to have clinched the matter by holding back his mother's deathbed letter which reveals Tom to be not a foundling but his half-brother.

All one could say for Blifil is that, like Boswell with his Scottishness, he cannot help it. He is the victim of his nature. In his bid for Sophia's hand he is entirely free from the passion of love, 'yet was he altogether as well furnished with other passions, that promised themselves very full gratification in the young lady's fortune. Such were avarice and ambition, which divided the dominion of his mind between them' (*Tom Jones,* I, p. 286). Driven by these vices, and in addition feeling for Sophia 'the same desires which an ortolan inspires into the soul of an epicure' (*Tom Jones,* I, p. 354), Blifil 'intended to deceive Sophia, by pretending love to her; and to deceive her father and his own uncle, by pretending he was beloved by her,' using for support the opposing theories of the two domestic scholars, Thwackum and Square (*Tom Jones,* I, p.355). Nothing in Blifil commands sympathy. He is as bad as Wild, although less violent. Even in defeat he remains hard and repellent, shedding the wrong sort of tears: not contrite tears that 'wash away guilt from minds which have been surprised or seduced into it unawares, against the bent of their natural dispositions, as will sometimes happen to human frailty, even to the good: no, these tears were such as the frighted thief sheds in his cart, and are indeed the effects of that concern which the most savage natures are seldom deficient in feeling for themselves' (*Tom Jones,* III, p. 356).

Blifil is unvaryingly cold and mean, no more capable of a generous act than the majority of characters in *Joseph Andrews.* If he seems worse than they are, that is partly because of his large share in the story, and partly because of his criminal act in withholding the letter; but it is also because he operates frighteningly on his own. In *Joseph Andrews* the wicked encourage and fortify each other, as it were; seeing each other in action, they can almost be forgiven for thinking that theirs is the way of the world. Blifil receives no support of this kind. The Allworthy and Western households are largely on his side only because they have been taken in by him, not because they feel the same way. Between Tom and Sophia at one extreme, and Blifil at the other, there is a complex series of transitional gradations in the novel. Between the mentality of Joseph and that of Scout or Trulliber, an abyss yawns; between those of Tom and Blifil, the land is densely populated. Dowling for instance, the lawyer who acts as Blifil's accomplice, is a reprehensible character but he is not, like Scout, a small Iago. When we hear Dowling trying to talk his way out of his involvement in Blifil's shame, he sounds painfully human. " 'Your Worship,' answered he, 'must remember that you were at that time ill in bed; and being in a violent hurry, as indeed I always am, I delivered the letter and message to Mr Blifil ...' " (*Tom Jones,* III,

p. 334). This only shows once again, as Fielding explains on the next page, that 'it is possible for a man to convey a lie in the words of the truth.' Dowling is not an honest man; but we know how he must feel, as we never did with Scout.

Evil takes on a human appearance in *Tom Jones*. Lord Fellamar could not possibly be the reader's friend, with his ambition to take Sophia away from Jones, and he is perhaps rather a barren soul; but again, we can feel sorry for the poor man, tempted out of his depth by Lady Bellaston's misjudgment. Young Nightingale, who suffers Tom's moral censure when he decides to leave the Miller girl after deliberately winning her love, marries her a little later, and there is no suggestion that this is purely a victory of principle. Black George the gamekeeper, who steals the £500 given to Tom by Allworthy, feels great pleasure when he can help him by delivering a letter, and is 'as honest as men who love money better than any other thing in the universe generally are' (*Tom Jones*, I, p.322).

Similar gradations occur among the women. Mrs Western, in spite of being a staunch supporter of her brother's design to get Sophia married for money, is as human as anybody's sister when she explains to Western that everything that goes wrong is always his fault. ' "Why, you are to blame, brother," answered she, "I have often been obliged to tell you so. However, I hope you will now amend ..." ' (*Tom Jones*, III, p. 215). Even Lady Bellaston is not unpardonable. Lady Booby, when she was trying to seduce Joseph Andrews, had only a white neck to recommend her in the author's eyes; none of her words and deeds were reported with sympathy or compassion. Lady Bellaston, in a comparable situation, does rather better. She has Tom's company at night for a time; and when she writes feverish letters to him followed by three P.S.'s (*Tom Jones*, III, p. 96), and proposes a further meeting at the end of a furious note refusing his offer of marriage (*Tom Jones*, III, p. 179), she has a distinct presence in the novel as a woman, not as a caricature of one.

Comparing the relationship between Joseph and Lady Booby with that between Tom and Lady Bellaston is enough to reveal a major difference between the moral attitudes of the two books. The former stay firmly apart; the latter grow towards each other, with Tom committing a fault far beneath Joseph, and Lady

Bellaston being sufficiently humanized to make Lady Booby green with envy.

The moral distinctions have become blurred, or more complex. And then *Amelia* follows.

iv

Although *Amelia* has been treated extensively and fairly by many critics it is surely true that it is generally regarded as a falling-off after *Tom Jones,* and is little read outside the circles of people who are interested in the whole of Fielding's oeuvre. Reasons for this are easy to find. *Amelia* is a less self-assured and enterprising novel than the two preceding ones. It has little comedy; it hangs around London with hardly any visible background; there is such a pervasive sadness in it that by the time the good are rewarded and the bad punished we are past cheering up; and most importantly for the present argument, it marks a further stage in the blurring of moral distinctions.

Not that Amelia herself has anything wrong with her except for a damaged nose that Fielding had given her, untactfully in the days of the pox. Amelia is moral beauty incarnate, and her husband Booth is not far behind, although at the beginning of the story he has a renewal of an old love-affair with Miss Matthews in prison, and although in Book X he turns out to be an occasional compulsive gambler. He is bound to strike most readers as a tedious man, well-meaning but with nothing much in him except for a justifiable feeling that he is giving his wife a hard time, through his frequent absences when he is detained by the bailiff for debts.

Although *Amelia*, as has often been pointed out and commented,[18] under the influence of *Clarissa* comes much closer to Richardson's vision than would have seemed possible ten years earlier, and there is a great deal about humble meals in the home and little about inns, Booth and Amelia are the same sort of people as Fielding's earlier good characters. They stand for good nature

---

18. To name two: Ian Watt, *The Rise of the Novel,* p. 92; and C.J. Rawson, *Henry Fielding and the Augustan Ideal under Stress,* p. 96.

and a healthy and happy love life, and they mostly sound too good to be true.

One characteristic of Fielding's pure lovers is that they never express their feelings in other than inflated terms. In *Joseph Andrews* and *Tom Jones* this matters less than in *Amelia,* because there everybody talks in heightened rhetorical prose most of the time; but now there is an awkward contrast occasionally with the drier and more lifelike tones of the other characters. As Amelia's virtue is unsuccessfully threatened by a succession of admirers one gradually loses interest in how she will react. She will never find anyone attractive unless they are kind to her children or are prepared to help the family financially. One is possibly a little more intrigued by her husband who is not quite so untouchable, but in the end he too is a disappointment.

The interest in this book does not lie with the wicked either, who are invisible most of the time. Miss Harris, Amelia's sister, makes an early appearance in the story but is virtually forgotten by the time we hear how she managed to keep her mother's inheritance out of Amelia's hands. As for the nameless noble lord whose lust threatens not really Amelia's virtue but certainly her peace of mind, he does not sound too bad on the few occasions when we meet him, and he goes out of his way to answer her requirement of kindness to the children. Although there is something repulsive about his technique of winning the mother's favour through the children it has an amateurish quality as well, particularly when it does not get him anywhere. There is no doubt that Fielding dislikes him and it is no surprise when in the concluding chapter he sends him to an unsavoury death from venereal disease; at the same time one should realize that a man of his disposition would have looked much more consistently vicious in *Joseph Andrews.*

Even at a point near the extreme of human wickedness the noble peer illustrates Fielding's tendency to admit more contradiction in his treatment of moral character. In this case we are limited to a few passing moments of doubt what judgment we are invited to form. In other cases the uncertainty is more persistent. Colonel James, Mrs James, Colonel Bath, Mrs Ellison, Mrs Bennet who becomes Mrs Atkinson, Captain Trent: in the last resort we may be in no doubt where to place these natures on the moral scale, but on the way there it is often possible to see them from different angles at the same time. It is only partially a question of good and evil.

Bath is obviously not too bad: but is he impossible and silly or unpleasant and gruff? James is no better than he ought to be: but is he a man of good will harrassed by strange urges, or an egomaniac softened by occasional good intentions? Mrs Bennet or Atkinson seems a basically good girl who has been through hard times, yet it is difficult to trust her when she tells the story of her life, and one needs to think carefully what the rights and wrongs of the case are when she impersonates Amelia as an act of friendship but makes use of the situation to get a commission for her husband (*Amelia*, II, pp. 230-3). Trent was plainly unscrupulous in the way he sold his wife to the noble lord; but instead of radiating viciousness from a mile away he is presented to us as a perfectly amicable drinking companion from whom we would only gradually begin to feel compelled to withdraw our assent if he insisted on unfolding his mercenary principles (*Amelia*, II, pp. 221-3).

It would not be true to say that Fielding is unclear in his judgment of any of these characters; although perhaps he was not absolutely certain of it either. Twenty years ago John S. Coolidge, who was struck particularly with the merits of Mrs Atkinson's characterization, wrote that in the process of creating her Fielding 'developed a conception of the relation between good and evil which challenges that represented by his Amelia.'[19] Possibly this conception was not fully developed at this stage. Robert Alter, quoting Coolidge with respect, may be more accurate when he says of the characterization of Colonel James that it 'would appear to point toward complexities and ambiguities which Fielding himself was not quite ready to confront or follow out.'[20] At a further remove from praise, although not entirely disapproving either, we find C.J. Rawson saying that it looks as if 'Fielding's world has ceased to make total sense, so that his reactions have become fragmentary.'[21]

In any case, Fielding leaves us to determine the exact weight we want to give to each of his judgments. It is our business to decide whether we will or will not have the living examples of James and Trent and Mrs Atkinson as friends, knowing what they are like. It

19. John S. Coolidge, 'Fielding and "Conservation of Character,"' *Mod. Phil.*, XVII no. 4 (1960), 245-259.
20. Robert Alter, *Fielding and the Nature of the Novel*, p. 157.
21. Rawson, *Henry Fielding and the Augustan Ideal under Stress*, p. 96.

would not have occurred to us to invite people like Wild an Blifil, Trulliber and Scout into our homes. The Jameses however, and Trent and Mrs Atkinson, may have been there for all we know, without quite revealing all their practices. They are not beyond the pale. The wicked have become socially acceptable, although wickedness remains as objectionable as ever.

Logically the process of socialization of the bad would demand a corresponding movement towards the middle ground of the good. There is in fact a little of that, in Adams and Tom Jones and in Booth, but it never gets to a stage where we could be in doubt what to think of them. They remain too good to be true. No human being is quite as unworldly as Adams, as charming as Tom, or as harmless as Booth. And yet: there are signs of irritability in the Booth household from time to time that might in further novels have led to quarrels, and then to a more balanced view of the good as well as the bad. Everybody knows or should know that while some people manage to give signs of friendliness and generosity more frequently than others, they are inevitably heterogeneous compositions like the rest. Really beautiful natures do not exist except in fits and starts. The conditions of human existence will not allow them continuity, and the state of perpetual serenity that the Wilsons enjoyed and the Joneses and the Booths were looking forward to cannot be more than an illusion for us, and a somewhat oppressive one at that.

The pull of the sense of reality in life and literature is mostly towards a recognition of these basic facts of experience; but not entirely. Not only will authors tend to prefer some characters to others; however much they may be against idealization of vice and virtue, story-telling normally requires a degree of partiality from an author. Sceptical though the novelist may be of rights and wrongs in human relations, the reader's sympathies need a focus some- where, in fictional situations as much as they do in real ones. It is in this context that moral good and bad function in the novel. No reader may want novelists to tell him how to behave or how to tell friends and children to behave, but we do expect to be on some people's side in their confrontations with outsiders or with fortune.

A difference between life and literature that has to be taken into account is that in reality we are not in the habit of checking on people's morality before becoming friends with them, or choosing their side. Although extreme conflicts of moral principle can make friendship impossible, in details of conduct we tend to choose our friends' side, right or wrong. Friendship often precedes judgment, and this is all the more inescapable as a condition of life because our own standards may leave something to be desired so that we could not pick and choose even if we knew how to do it.

In literature this does not apply. Readers have traditionally been invited to be on the side of the good. In most cases they still are, even though the eighteenth-century idea that the arts and the novel had the duty to serve the cause of virtue is no longer commonly accepted. After two-and-a-half centuries there is a different idea, or plurality of ideas, about the purpose of the novel, and in the works of Graham Greene or Iris Murdoch we are by no means always invited to be on the side of the good. The basic expectation remains nonetheless the same. It belongs inevitably to the art of story-telling. Tension is created by giving us the hope that something desirable may happen, and the fear that it may not. If we correctly imagine modern novel production to consist largely of detective stories, love stories, and stories of adventure on earth and in the universe, the purpose of the novel looks pleasantly simple. It is only in the thin air near the top, where the intellectuals and trendsetters demand new forms and difficulties, that this simple principle is twisted into unusual shapes.

The intellectuals have a point, however. There has always been something false about the enthusiasm novelists and readers pretended to share for the good. Why should people expect stricter observation of rules of conduct when reading than when leading their own lives? The most likely explanation of the phenomenon is that as listeners to stories they have learned to see in the good a signal indicating which side they have to be on to ensure participation in the pleasure of winning, or the emotion of losing. That, they know, is how things work in the world of the imagination. It is not life. It's only a story.

It is an attempt to get away from oversimplification and boredom that has led to the introduction of more complex relationships between good and bad in the novel. It is also, in a more developed sense of the word, a moral urge: a desire for greater honesty than can be shown by a reader who uses books to get away from the moral complexities of the real world.

In Fielding's novels we can see the simple and complex moralities both at work, with the simple one's pure goodness losing ground but remaining dominant. The position of his heroes and heroines was made unassailable by his notion that only the good and pure can be happy in love. The wicked, the vicious and the unpleasant lack the generosity to enjoy their loves. They lead the chilly barren lives of people outside our circles, the people we ignore and disapprove of. The Wilsons and Joneses and Booths live inside: they are our sort of people, decent and often dull, and we are familiar with their manners and their jokes.

Except that they overdo it, falling on their knees too often and letting their rhetoric get out of control. Belonging to the eighteenth century is insufficient excuse for the way they go on. Many writers of the period, Defoe and Sterne to name two, were nowhere near as insistent on the purity and happiness of their protagonists. Fielding's people are pleasant to look at, and the account of their adventures remains enjoyable for a variety of reasons, but the insistence on the excellence of his favourites becomes counter-productive in the end. Instead of feeling stimulated to let our own good nature shine forth more brilliantly than it normally does, we tend to smile indulgently. These are storybook figures; they make no difference.

And then Fielding's moral seriousness, which mostly manifested itself in discursive passages in the earlier books, breaks out in his characterization as well, and suspends our smile. It is perhaps impossible to know to what extent he did it consciously, in the story for instance of Booth's indignation when the maid Betty has stolen some of Amelia's clothes. Just before this happened, poor Amelia had had to pawn most of her clothes, so as to raise the money to pay the gambling debts incurred by Booth in a weak moment. 'Booth now declared that he would go in pursuit of little Betty, against whom he vowed so much vengeance, that Amelia endeavoured to moderate his anger by representing to him the girl's youth, and that this was the first fault she had ever been guilty of' (*Amelia,* II, p. 270).

It seems almost impossible to read about Booth's heated indignation without thinking that he is transferring his own guilt on to someone else; but did Fielding think so, consciously? When Betty is brought before the court the J.P. sounds sorry to be unable to convict her, as the value of the stolen goods is under forty shillings; and Booth gives further vent to his indignation in terms which are much like Fielding's own ideas on criminal law (see below, p. 145). There is no sign that Fielding felt at all ambiguous about Booth's response to the discovery of the theft. Yet this outburst provokes puzzled surprise and suspicion in the modern reader, and it would seem absurd to think that that could never have happened in the eighteenth-century. It seems just possible though that Fielding, in the heat of writing, was not aware of the implication — rather like his not foreseeing the scurrilous laughter he would excite with Amelia's damaged nose.

Whether intentionally or not, *Amelia* is greatly enriched by scenes like this one of Booth, by Colonel James offering to put up Booth's bail and then withdrawing the offer because he wants Mrs Booth and would rather keep the husband in prison (*Amelia*, II, pp. 101-3); by Mrs Ellison perfectly coherently explaining that prudery gets you nowhere (*Amelia*, I, p. 20); by Mrs Bennet getting mixed up and saying 'I am so confused ... that I scarcely know what I say; yes, yes, I remember I did say so ...' (*Amelia*, I, p. 320). It is tempting to think of these things as happening without Fielding having worked out the intention and the effect — simply because this was where his desire to represent real people took him. The point is not essential, however, to the appreciation of the scenes themselves, which justify a view of *Amelia* as being in this respect the best of Fielding's novels.

This judgment will probably only make sense for readers who answer two requirements. They will have to agree that the moral significance of a novel does not depend on the number of shining youths incarnating the author's idea of all the major virtues and rewarded with lifelong serenity. This must be taken to be only a narrative ploy; and moral values do not enter the discussion until we see characters divided between impulses, and become aware of the alternatives confronting them, including the temptation simply to do what is most convenient because life is a mess anyway. The other requirement is a willingness to allow that novels which are feeble in some ways can be powerful in others. *Amelia* has more than its fair share of overstatement and underorganization, which means that many passionate pronouncements remain without effect and that many narrative details are superfluous and forgettable.

Nor does *Amelia* have much of the comedy and the humour of *Joseph Andrews* and *Tom Jones*. What it does offer is a number of dramatized views of human ambiguity and complexity which, both in themselves and as previews of the development of the novel, are little miracles. Out of the silence of the past there come these voices, not at all pleasant sometimes, but alive. To the extent that Fielding's work relies on his earlier moral teaching for its significance, it does not mean much; it is only near the end, when the clear direction was lost, that he begins to affect our perception of human conduct.

II THE HUMORIST

'What is most memorable about Fielding,' as Martin Battestin writes before setting out on his analysis of the moral basis of *Joseph Andrews,* 'is not his morality or his religion, but his comedy — the warm breath of laughter that animates his fiction.'[1] This judgment will not encounter much opposition. We all tend to think of Fielding's novels in terms of mad pursuits through unspoilt countrysides studded with old-fashioned inns, of noisy battles with kitchen utensils between characters oddly or inadequately dressed, of insults phrased with perfect grammatical control, and of expansive eighteenth-century gestures. Nor does Fielding himself try to argue us out of our view of him as a comic writer. *Joseph Andrews* was going to be 'a comic epic poem in prose,' he announced in the Preface, which meant that it would contain characters 'of inferior rank,' but also that it would in 'its fable and action' concern itself with the 'light and ridiculous.' Even in the 'fifties, a few months after the publication of *Amelia,* when Fielding discussed the 'scope and end of reading' in an essay for the last of his four short-lived newspapers, he had a good word for laughter:

'for why', as Horace says, 'should not any one promulgate truth with a smile on his countenance? Ridicule, indeed,' as he again intimates,' is commonly stronger and better method of attacking vice than the severer kind of satire.'[2]

There can be no doubt that Fielding's sense of humour was too strong to desert him entirely even in his sad last days. At the same time his words confirm the impression gained earlier that it would be a destructive act to separate the novelist in him from the humorist. The latter's main task was to serve the cause of the former.

Although it would be too sweeping to claim that the comedy is always subservient to the morality, one can say that it operates

1. Martin C. Battestin, *The Moral Basis of Fielding's Art,* p.x.
2. *Covent Garden Journal,* no. 10, quoted in Ioan Williams (ed.), *The Criticism of Henry Fielding,* p. 159.

independently only on privileged occasions. The well-known scene when Adams visits his fellow clergyman Trulliber for instance, in order to borrow a badly needed small sum of money, is severe in its condemnation of the host. When Adams complying with Trulliber's requirement enters the pigsty and touches one of the pigs 'the unruly beast gave such a sudden spring that he threw poor Adams all along in the mire' (*Joseph Andrews*, p. 188). In itself, this could be harmless fun, for the reader if not for Adams; but it is not left to itself. Trulliber, in his refusal to lend the small sum, reveals a mean and coarse nature that demands our disapproval, and moreover forces us to recognize a clear contrast between his moral quality and that of Adams. The fun was not harmless after all. It was uncharitable greed in action, and the scene leaves us tense with judgment rather than relaxed with laughter.

A similar comment can be made on one of the great comic *tableaux* of *Tom Jones*: the discovery of the philosopher Square, undressed, behind a rug in Molly's bedroom. It is a moment of great relief to Tom, who was afraid that his honour required him to remain faithful for life to poor Molly. The revelation in the bedroom frees him to concentrate on Sophia, and we have every reason to join in the 'immoderate laughter' Fielding thinks any spectator would have produced; but there is a moral lesson as well, telling us that philosophers are flesh and blood like the rest of us, and that deists can use their concept of *natural law* to talk their way out of anything, arguing with Square that: 'Fitness is governed by the nature of things, and not by customs, forms or municipal laws. Nothing is indeed unfit which is not unnatural' (*Tom Jones*, I, p. 230). We may laugh immoderately, but there is no relaxation of the rules.

It is in the spirit of the same rules that we should not in general be invited to laugh at our favourites. Parson Adams is the exception; we are not told to take him seriously whatever he does. Tom Jones, with all his good nature, is not really a comic hero so much as a *jeune premier;* and Fanny, Sophia and Amelia, although reliable girls and very pretty, form an unfunny trio. The only time anyone may be tempted to laugh at Sophia is on her arrival at a 'very fair promising inn' when she falls on top of the landlord who is helping her to dismount from her horse. Bystanders display an 'immoderate grin'; Fielding, not entirely seriously but very firmly, tells us what the proper reaction is: '... nor will we scruple to say that he must have a very inadequate idea of the modesty of a beautiful young woman who could wish to sacrifice it to so paltry a satisfaction as can arise from laughter' (*Tom Jones*, II, p. 251).

In the rest of Fielding's fiction, *Jonathan Wild* with its rigid irony is naturally devoid of relaxed comedy. So is *Amelia*, in its sombre view of eighteenth-century manners. When Jenny Bath becomes stand-offish after her marriage to Colonel James (*Amelia*, I, pp. 208-9) or when Amelia mixes things up and imagines Mrs Ellison has married Sergeant Atkinson (*Amelia*, I, pp. 289-90), or when the buck finds Dr Harrison's letter on chastity at the masquerade and reads it aloud (*Amelia*, II, pp. 188-92), the occasion may provoke a hesitant laugh which the judicious reader suppresses before it can open out, realizing that the point is not in the comedy.

The only part of Fielding's fiction where laughter can be quite unrestrained is *Shamela*, which is a special case because the fictional character here is not a comment on human nature but on another fictional character. The treatment of Shamela is comparable to the adding of moustaches and the blacking-out of teeth on advertising posters, and immoderate grins are in order.

To say that Fielding's comedy mostly serves his morality does not necessarily define its value either upwards or downwards. Some people feel that the best comedy should be supported by strong moral preferences and therefore tend towards the satirical; for others a better variety occurs when the categories of order and logic and consistency are broken up, provided the results are not too disastrous. The superiority of one kind or the other is all the more difficult to demonstrate because it depends on one's mood in its variations from day to day. What one can venture to say without too much prejudice is that non-committal humour at its best is funnier than the satiric kind, for the simple reason of its purity. Even in Swift, whose satiric powers are beyond dispute, no more delightful scene occurs than when little Gulliver plays the spinet for the royal couple of Brobdingnag, running up and down in front of the keyboard and hitting the keys with muffled cudgels. However highly one may think of Swift's ridiculing of ministerial selection or nationalist sentiment or Royal Society experimentation, none of those passages possess the irresistible quality of the musical performance.

It will be worth considering whether the same can be said in the case of Fielding. Certainly he offers opportunities for comparing the different kinds of humour. Although he mostly goes in for the satiric kind, he has memorable passages where no questions of condemnation and alternatives arise. When Adams wades through a pool of water without noticing the footpath leading round it, and when Western forgets his apparently single-minded pursuit of Sophia and joins a hunt which crosses his path, there is no judgment involved (*Joseph Andrews,* p. 110, and *Tom Jones,* II, p. 306). There is only observation of human nature in action, bringing a soothing sense that the irrationality of our conduct is a charm rather than a danger.

It is true that all these examples are of visual physical comedy. For the sake of argument one could imagine Fielding being more relaxed and more willing to allow non-committal comedy in his comment than in his descriptive passages. The argument would not detain us very long. If anything Fielding is stricter in his treatment of ideas than of events. His irony is usually of the stable type, in Wayne Booth's terminology:[3] he refers clearly to the right principles when he says something contrary or out of proportion to them. 'Be it known then, that the human species are divided into two sorts of people, to wit, high people and low people' (*Joseph Andrews*, p. 180); — 'As the love which Blifil had for Sophia was of that violent kind which nothing but the loss of her fortune, or some such accident, could lessen' (*Tom Jones,* III, p. 227), are typical examples. Much of the irony of *Joseph Andrews* and *Tom Jones* is as rigorous as anything in *Jonathan Wild.*

Yet here too, exceptions occur. A clear view of Fielding's comedy will not be achieved unless we subdivide it into different kinds, while realizing that these do not represent him playing separate games, but shade into each other as expressions of the author in various moods and situations. If this is taken into account, it will be helpful so split up the humour of Fielding's work into five classes: 1) the purely verbal fun, 2) the knockabout comedy, 3) the satire, 4) the character-comedy and 5) the personal irony. Further subdivisions, while possible, would only increase the difficulty of recognizing any of the different types during the actual reading of the work.

The precise classification matters less than the awareness of

3. Wayne C. Booth, *A Rhetoric of Irony,* pp. 5-7.

different kinds of humour, dependent on different ways of viewing the world, and by no means equal in the power to make us laugh. It may be useful to start with the realization that Fielding was not primarily a funny man at all. He has his funny moments, but they are nowhere near as frequent as for instance Sterne's, nor do they dominate his world picture to the same extent. Sterne's imagination was continually tickled by new absurdities and comic conceits that occurred to him; his humour was private in origin, although fortunately for us he developed into a successful show-off as he grew older.

Not so Fielding, who always sounds far more like a public man — an entertainer, whose best ideas come when he imagines his audience waiting for him. Again, this is not always true. There are moments when his humour seems more concerned with his own amusements, such as the one early in *Joseph Andrews* when he tells us that Joseph's appointment as Jack o'Lent had to be terminated because his lovely voice charmed the birds out of the trees instead of frightening them away. Not that this is a very secretive joke compared to some of Sterne's, but its absurd literalness comes at a moment in the book when we are not prepared for such liberties, and suggests an author enjoying himself rather than trying to persuade an audience.

Usually Fielding is more audience-conscious than that. He sounds as if he is talking to us as a group, not indulging in intimate banter whose point might be lost on most of us, but basing his performance on ideas that we might broadly be expected to share with him and with each other. Our reaction to this approach is only to a small extent determined by the discovery of peculiarities in human conduct and thinking; much more of it consists of relief and reassurance at finding ourselves holding the right end of the stick, entitled to merriment at the expense of the twisters at the other end.

If Fielding had nothing else to offer us we could not expect much pleasure out of him after two centuries, but once he has established a relationship with his audience he goes on to practice his other kinds of humour. It may seem rash to try and indicate some of these. E.B. White, quoted by George R. Levine in his book on Fielding's irony, was right to warn us against dissecting humour and expecting it to stay alive.[4] However, the same can be

4. George R. Levine, *Henry Fielding and the Dry Mock,* p.7.

said of most criticism. Only a few privileged critics succeed in showing up the shapes and contours of a literary landscape; more often it is flattened into a map. The risk has to be accepted.

ii

The thinnest variety of Fielding's humour occurs when he tries his hand at classical and heroic pastiche.

> Now the rake Hesperus had called for his breeches, and having well rubbed his drowsy eyes, prepared to dress himself for all night; ... In vulgar language, it was in the evening when Joseph attended his lady's orders (*Joseph Andrews*, p. 47).

Such passages make one imagine Fielding laughing before anyone else. They require no comic observation, only a knack of continuing in a well-established tradition of comic pastiche. There is a touch of snobbery in them which has lost most of its effect. Originally they would have appealed most to readers 'as scholarly and as much interested in literary theory as Richardson's public was interested in sex, money and social success.'[5] The people Fielding expected as readers, unlike those of the common romances of the time and of Defoe and Richardson, were expected to have had a proper literary schooling. There are times when it causes a passing surprise to find the man who spoke so slightingly of the distinction between high and low people assuming such a qualification in his sort of public.[6] The surprise should not be taken seriously. It is falsely ingenuous, as if such contradictions did not belong to human beings.

Fielding was probably animated less by sympathy with those of elementary Latin training than by a dislike of those without it who imagined they were just as good. This anti-egalitarianism would put him on the side of Pope and Swift and other scourges of dulness, with whom he felt at home. It is one of the characteristics of *Amelia* that although it completely lacks the mock heroic passages that belong to the insouciance of the preceding two books, it dispenses with Latin quotations only for a time. When Dr. Harrison finally produces two of them in a letter they are

5. Gilbert Highet, *The Classical Tradition*, p. 342.
6. cf. H.K. Miller, *Essays on Fielding's Miscellanies*, pp. 100-2 and n. 81.

helpfully translated at the bottom of the page. By the time Mrs Bennet astonishes Booth by quoting six lines from Virgil as part of a conversation, the translation service has been stopped (*Amelia*, I, pp. 155 and 310). Although a changed man in some ways, Fielding was still no educational egalitarian.

In the happier days of the 1740s there was never any question of footnotes for the Latin quotations, beyond an occasional translation by 'Mr Pope' offered as part of the text. The reader's Latin should be good enough to enable him to savour the English equivalent; and classic and translations would recall his schooldays, so that the proper response was not so much laughter as the chuckle of the old boys' dinner.[7]

The reference of the mock heroic passages was not exclusively to the classics. They could also be set beside the eighteenth century's own tragic style, which in his younger days as a dramatist Fielding had taken off with good effect in *Tom Thumb*. Its weaknesses and affectations were asking to be parodied, and the result can be mildly amusing even if we ourselves have not been bothered by the originals. Some passages are relatively straightforward:

O vanity! how little is thy force acknowledged, or thy operations discerned ... Avarice is often no more than thy handmaid, and even lust thy pimp, ...

which we might take in our stride if it were not for the different note at the end:

... for know, to thy confusion, that I have introduced thee the panegyric on vanity for no other purpose than to lengthen out a short chapter, ... (*Joseph Andrews*, pp. 82-3).

Some are more florid:

As in the month of June, the damask rose, which chance has planted among the lilies, with their candid hue mixes his vermilion; or, as some playsome heifer in the pleasant month of May diffuses her odoriferous breath over the flowery meadows; ... (*Tom Jones*, II, p. 212).

7. Or, in a few cases, the delight of the connoisseur, if the reader was a classical scholar like A.D. Leeman who has indicated the original passages in Virgil, Statius and Seneca of four bits of pastiche in *Tom Jones*, Book VIII, ch.ix, adding that only the reader who knows his classics could fully appreciate such a passage. V. *Lampas* 1,1 (1968), 24.

There is no particular harm in this, but the expenditure of comic energy seems wasteful in proportion to the product.

The idea that classical quotations and allusions are expressive of a streak of snobbery can be confirmed by a closer look at the role of Partridge, the former schoolmaster and barber who accompanies Tom Jones on his journey. There is much to be said for Partridge as a character. He has that exclusive quality of seeming a person of more interest than his author appears to consider him. One of his oddities is a predilection for Latin quotations not out of Virgil and Horace like those of his betters, but out of a standard grammar, and not always appropriate. There is little doubt that Fielding holds the low level of Partridge's education against him, and treats him as a Grub Street schoolmaster. He is a human being of a lower order than his employer. Only on rare occasions does he get any credit for his Sancho Panza-like contributions to the novel.

One could argue that the most important of his comic turns, when he has the star role in the theatre auditorium at a performance of *Hamlet,* should compensate him for the humiliations elsewhere. Certainly his inability to distinguish properly between life on the stage and in reality, and his lack of respect for Shakespeare's characterization, are presented as eminently amusing, with the endorsement of the audience. He hardly shuts up during the performance, and one would expect extreme annoyance at least among those in the nearest seats; but to them most of all, it appears afterwards, he had 'afforded great mirth,' and they had been 'more attentive to what he said than to anything that passed on the stage' (*Tom Jones,* III, p. 226). It would still not be true to say that Partridge has been redeemed by this outburst of audience participation. A performing monkey could count on the same sort of appreciation. He remains a barber and a schoolmaster and worse, a bad Latinist. He is not, by Fielding's standards, our class of person.

iii

With his elementary Latin, Partridge's place is among Fielding's jokes of verbal imitation; with his behaviour, on this as on other occasions, he takes part in the knockabout comedy. Among general as opposed to specialized readers Fielding is better known for this aspect of his work than for any other, which in a way is unfair to him, because he shows more originality and inventiveness in other respects, and as a novelist he was emphatic about his wish to keep away from or elevate himself above mere burlesque. On the other hand, Cervantes who was his revered master had been by no means averse to farcical scenes; and Fielding did not put them in only because he felt he owed it to convention.

The farcical scenes, with a great deal of noisy action and little concern for characterization, belong to his view of life. One could specify this further by saying that it applies both externally and internally. The external side is the commotion and the noise these scenes cause. There is a good reason for thinking that Fielding enjoyed audible assertions of life. If novels actually produced the sounds they described there would be no noisier books in the language than *Joseph Andrews* and *Tom Jones*. In the latter particularly, noisy incidents are rife. Sophia had hardly finished telling Harriet Fitzpatrick about recent events when they heard 'a noise, not unlike, in loudness, to that of a pack of hounds just let out from their kennel' (*Tom Jones,* II, p. 283). When Tom was engaged in conversation with the master of the travelling puppet-show, 'A violent uproar now arose in the entry, ...' (II, p. 323); in London, talking to Mrs Fitzpatrick, he 'had scarce finished his story when a most violent noise shook the whole of the house' (III, p. 45); and after an emotional evening with Mrs Miller talking about her daughter whose lover has deserted her, he might have slept until midday 'had not a violent uproar awakened him' (III, p. 116). When Lord Fellamar's friend has talked to Mr Western, not only does the Squire send 'many curses and some menaces after him,' but Sophia, upstairs, 'began now first to thunder with her foot, and afterwards to scream as loudly as the old gentleman himself had done before ...' (III, p. 204). When Mrs Miller is talking to Mr Allworthy, a violent knocking at the door interrupted their conversation ... (III, p. 252).

The assaults on the reader's aural imagination usually herald some new arrival or development, and are perfectly functional in the story. This is not to say that the story would have been hard put to proceed without them in much the same way. Taking into account the frequent noises in Fielding, the violence and bitterness, however comical, of the emotions he ascribes to his characters, and the loudness of many of their exchanges, he can justly be thought a novelist who likes noise for its dramatic narrative effect.

As characterization, the knockabout scenes can often be related to Fielding's gloomy view of human nature. Cheerful entertainer though he might be, his characters in the main are mean and intolerant types. It causes no surprise when they start throwing things at each other. They are not particularly strong or vicious, nor are they well armed, so while they make a mess of things they cause no serious injury; but once we have excepted the heroes and heroines and a few ageing advisers, they all look tight-lipped. We laugh at them because of the clumsiness of their battle, not for the spirit in which it is fought:

> Molly pursued her victory, and catching up a skull which lay on the side of a grave, discharged it with such fury that, having hit a tailor on the head, the two skulls sent equally forth a hollow sound at their meeting, and the tailor took presently measure of his length on the ground, where the skulls lay side by side, and it was doubtful which was the more valuable of the two.

Although undeniably a piece of comic writing, this uses too much violence to put us at our ease, and Fielding sensibly introduced a piece of mock-classical writing to ensure laughter:

> Recount, O Muse, the names of those who fell on this fatal day ... old Echepole ... received a blow in his forehead ...Kate of the mill tumbled unfortunately over a tombstone ... Betty Pippin, with young Roger her lover, fell both to the ground, where, O perverse fate! she salutes the earth, and he the sky (*Tom Jones,* I, pp. 171-2).

The comedy is unmistakable, culminating in the mildly obscene perception of the last sentence, but the strain remains. Similar ambiguous moods were generated by the fights in *Joseph Andrews.* When Adams and Joseph are attacked by a pair of hounds while the huntsman looks on roaring with laughter, Fielding also called in the classics: 'Now thou, whoever thou art, whether a muse, or by what other name soever thou choosest to be called, who presidest over biography, and hast inspired all the writers of lives in our times ....,' but the dogs' attack is not saved from viciousness (*Joseph Andrews,* p. 270). The eighteenth-century fun-lover's expectations were somewhat different from ours, and probably included more roughness in comedy than we are used to. Nonetheless one could not legitimately suspect Fielding of having found his fist-fights mere innocent diversions. Having taken Joseph and Adams and Fanny home with them for dinner, the squire and his friends proceed to inflict on the parson the practical joke which drops him from his seat into a tub of water (*Joseph Andrews,* pp. 283-4). This game has none of the charm of harmless fun.

The sense of humour that feeds on the pain and discomfort of victims is also shown in action in the few noisy scenes that occur in *Amelia,* particularly at the masquerade when one of the bucks finds Dr Harrison's letter in praise of chastity on the floor and reads it out to the crowd. There is no violent behaviour, but the mood suggested by Fielding's writing is one of disapproval and dislike. As in *Tom Jones,* 'a great noise arose' which 'was occasioned by a large assembly of young fellows whom they call bucks, who were got together, and were enjoying, as the phrase is, a letter, which one of them had found in the room' (*Amelia,* II, p. 188). No narrator could show less warmth for a group of characters. Between their mechanical glee and the lofty injunctions of the letter, there is no possibility of contact. Life is at a standstill; the night is filled with the meaningless cries of the vile multitude *sous le fouet du plaisir.* That is what happened when Fielding's farce and noise and knockabout fun were no longer surrounded by the movement and the zest for life of *Tom Jones.* The scenes themselves lost some of their animation; but in a book whose dominant mood was pained and poignant instead of exuberant like its predecessors, they would have looked uneasy in any case.

What the farcical scenes deserve to be remembered for is less their intrinsic merit than their role in relation to the rest of the novels. They provide variety in the narrative, which is a positive contribution, but they also change the moral vision. The dominant idea in Fielding's work is that the morality of readers can be corrected and cured, particularly by well-aimed laughs at their expense. It is the species not the individual that Fielding said he was addressing. Nonetheless, the species is represented by individuals in the novels, and the reader also acts as an individual. The reader receives private lessons in morality, which are to have their effect independently of social involvement. Next time he enters the world he will be a better person, if Horace was right.

There is no question of improving readers by describing to them those fights in kitchens and bedrooms and churchyards. Instead of impressing on us our capacity for improvement, they remind us that we are inextricably involved in social life. They do not just vary the moral vision of the book; they contradict it. Admittedly they do so in a crude form. Fielding has loaded the dice in favour of moral improvement; yet the knockabout scenes give those who want it the reassurance that unimproved liberty continues to exist, even though reprehensible and often not pleasant.

This reassurance does not only appear in the longer set pieces with their fighting and confusion. Brief farcical moments occur throughout the books, and help to keep the ragged flag of liberty flying. When they involve characters who are major presences in the story, they are often better placed under the headings of satire or character comedy; but not always even then, and there are plenty of minor characters in a strictly farcical vein. Tishy Snap who becomes Mrs Wild, several inn-keepers in both *Joseph Andrews* and *Tom Jones,* Lord Fellamar who tries to seduce Sophia, and Bondum the bailiff who expects civility-money from Booth on his release, are cases in point.

One could attempt to define all these and try to work out how much they each represent of the different types of humour, but that would be a labour of classification, not of appreciation. Between the main area are the transitional zones, and the more one compares them, the more complex everything becomes. There is a fine passage in *Jonathan Wild* where the hero, having been put off in a boat on his own by a gallant French captain decides to jump overboard but climbs back within two minutes, nature having whispered in his ear that she wants him to have further experiences. What is the meaning of this, if it must have one? Fielding's bitter philosophy, which argues that it is normal for greatness to exist in combination with unscrupulousness, could encourage us to take it seriously, and to adopt the view that in fact Nature (not to be confused with Good Nature) is our worst enemy, coldly resolved to behave like Fate.

Wild's self-rescue can be made to look pregnant with philosophic significance. It can also be regarded as a farcical incident: this man resolutely jumping overboard and thinking better of it almost immediately, although covering up for it with a piece of metaphysical speculation. As farce the passage is probably at its best, with a deadpan absurdity that would look well in a film of Buster Keaton. It seems to lend itself to various interpretations;

but in the end one remembers only an image, with numerous meanings none of which seem plausible on reflection. The image itself is the significant thing: a mystery in Fielding's work, irreducibly silent among the floods of comment and judgment.

iv

If Fielding's name evokes farcical comedy more than anything else for the general reader, for the academic reader it is primarily associated with satirical comedy, where his humour most explicitly serves the moral purpose which has helped him to live down the frowns of Dr Johnson and of his early biographers. This is where the two main streams of his genius meet and join up, and the opportunities for analysis and interpretation are endless.

Sometimes, it has to be admitted, a suspicion arises that there are moments when the morality serves the humour rather than the humour the morality. Was Fielding more concerned to admonish society or to make jokes about it? The most plausible answer is that his purpose depended on the situation and on his mood. He would not sacrifice his notion of right and wrong for a good laugh; on the other hand, having recognized that disapprobation can act as a stimulus to laughter, he was not above exploiting this aspect of human nature. On such occasions, we are meant not to waste our moral indignation, only to laugh at the way the world is being imposed on — the extreme example being *Shamela,* where the heroine is shown to have deceived even Richardson who invented her.

The extent to which Fielding believed that people might change for the better under the pressure of novelists and other moral counsellors remains difficult to define when one thinks of him primarily as a humorist, more concerned to laugh people out of their follies than to inspire them to better things. In his preface to *Joseph Andrews,* he wrote as if nothing could be easier to conceive than people being cured of their two forms of affectation: vanity and hypocrisy (*Joseph Andrews*, p. 22). This was by no means his last word on the subject. 'I believe, it is much easier to make good men wise, than to make bad men good,' he wrote in the Dedication of *Tom Jones.* Henry Knight Miller, discussing the contrasts in Fielding's pronouncements on the moral effects of literature, says that he 'escaped the dilemma by narrowing the sphere of his moral exhortations. As we have seen, his "theory" admitted the possibility of reform in natures not totally corrupted, but saw some men as possessed by ineradicable evil.[8]

With such distinctions in mind we can make sufficient sense of Fielding as the laughing moralist. The need to do so arises the sooner because he was never quite sweeping enough for a satirist. In some respects he seems a mere ironist, content to believe that the world will remain a confused and absurd place whatever rules we manage to apply. Swift might believe the same thing, but he allowed himself no contentment. He did not, like Fielding, enjoy much of life as it went on and save the dismay and melancholy for his summings-up; he burst into a fury as soon as anything happened.

Swift's surely was the true satiric spirit. This view is not incompatible with that of Wayne Booth when he opposes the notion that irony can only see the world as 'permanently unstable,' and that any attempt at correction comes under the heading of satire.[9] Booth's stable irony, which enables the ironist to make clear what he thinks preferable, is an indispensable intermediate form. When Swift disguises Sir Robert Walpole as Flimnap the Lilliputian minister who turns somersaults on a rope in order to keep his post, this is satire; when Fielding hides Walpole under the appellation of Great Man in various circumstances it is satiric irony, which condemns the man in the name of a different idea of greatness but tends to accept the wrong idea of it as belonging to the way the world thinks; if someone should call Walpole the Minister of Peace (which he was, but not in the state of secular sanctity that the epithet in isolation suggests), the irony would be pure or at least non-satirical, accepting the impossibility of making firm sense of a permanently unstable world.

Most of Fielding's satire is tempered with irony. Although he was a moralist with a message much of the time, he was too much of a novelist to flatten his characters entirely according to his book of rules. Unlike a pure satirist he did not relish the idea of making his victims look subhuman. One notices this when he is careful to point out in general terms that he is criticizing the species rather than the individual, but even more when he deals in particular with

8. Miller, *Essays on Fielding's Miscellanies*, p. 224.
9. Booth, *A Rhetoric of Irony*, pp. 92-3.

the individual who more memorably than anyone else incurred his displeasure, Colly Cibber. 'Lastly, how completely doth he arm us against so uneasy, so wretched, a passion as the fear of shame! how clearly doth he expose the emptiness and vanity of that phantom, reputation!' (*Joseph Andrews,* p. 26). By the ungentle standards of the 1740s this is mild stuff, inviting chuckles rather than the baring of teeth, particularly if one thinks of Cibber as a public figure who was doubtless of the persuasion that any publicity is better than none.

We have to look outside his fiction to find Fielding becoming really harsh and personal, as in the case of Mrs Francis who kept the inn at Ryde, whom he described in *The Voyage to Lisbon:* 'She was a short, squat woman; her head was closely joined to her shoulders, where it was fixed somewhat awry; every feature ... sharp and pointed; ... her complexion, which seemed to be able to turn the milk to curds ... resembled in colour such milk as had already undergone that operation' (p. 236) — and she was always complaining about the meanness of her customers.

Whatever the real Mrs Francis may have been like, it was cruel of Fielding to use her ugliness against her. Like Mrs Slipslop, she deserved our pity if nature's treatment of her had been so ungenerous, but he had little kindness to spare for unattractive women. One notices the same failing in him when he describes Goody Brown in her minor role in the churchyard fight with Molly and Tom Jones ('her bosom (if it may be so called), as well in colour as in many other properties, exactly resembling an ancient piece of parchment' — *Tom Jones,* I, p. 174). Such caricatures are farcical rather than satirical — got up for the occasion, not representative of an aspect of human nature.

The same applies to Blifil, although if he is to be called farcical it can only be in a black sense. Whatever one would call the object of the satirical exercise, whether the puncturing of affectation that Fielding wants or something else, nothing of the sort occurs in this case. From the moment we set eyes on him we can only see him as unpleasantness personified. When he tries a grand gesture and releases Sophia's bird which is immediately killed by a hawk; when he wants to prove that his heart in the right place by sympathizing with Allworthy over Tom's faults; when he assumes a considerate air and expresses a fear of offending Sophia, and when in his final defeat he throws himself on the ground before Tom — whatever he does and however he looks, he always fails to take us in.

Perhaps one thinks of him as a hero of melodrama rather than of farce, but the two are not far apart in our time which can no longer take melodramatic morals seriously. Trying to form an idea of a world that will most naturally accomodate characterizations like those of Blifil and Mrs Slipslop and Jonathan Wild and Shamela's parson Williams, one might conclude that it belongs typically to something definable as family satire. Inside our world there are ourselves and a few old friends whom we trust, although not necessarily forever; and then there is humanity outside, consisting of the foolish and the terrible and the awful, from whom it is always a relief to turn back to our own surroundings. 'How ridiculous,' we exclaim mechanically whenever new evidence of the differentness of others reaches us; and this is precisely what Fielding wanted us to say as readers. The family-satirical view of the world will never become definitive, and it is not always a happy one; but in the hands of a breezy entertainer like Fielding it turns into good fun, rich in characters whom we would nowadays describe as 'extraordinary' and 'mad', and with whom we easily form imaginary relationships.

The family-satirical view, founded in a defensive need for reassurance, cannot normally qualify as valid public satire. This is not to say that Fielding never gets as far as valid public satire at all, but his worst individuals are idiosyncratically bad instead of representatively so; one can laugh at them without having to counter any criticism of humanity as a whole, let alone of ourselves. The most unmistakably satirical passages deal with groups rather than individuals, or with characters standing for groups and not sharply defined in their own personalities. His doctors, lawyers, clergymen, beaux, inn-keepers and hack writers are mostly of no significance to us in their private capacity, and sometimes remain nameless; but as representatives of their professions and life styles they are pointedly criticized in the name of duty and generosity and good sense. As for groups present in their entirety, no better example could be quoted than the passengers of the stagecoach who are reluctant to help Joseph Andrews when he is found naked by the wayside, until a lawyer warns them that 'if he should die they might be called to some account for his murder' (*Joseph Andrews,* pp. 63-4; cf. above, p. 20). Here indeed we can recognize humanity in general, including ourselves; and similar effects are occasionally obtained with the summaries of public opinion in *Tom Jones.* When Allworthy is tolerant to Jenny who seems to have borne an illegitimate baby, public opinion thinks him too easy; when he sends her away out of the district it is rumoured that he himself is the father, and he is blamed for cruelty: once again we recognize our own world, and our ineradicable weakness (*Tom Jones,* I, pp. 44-5).

There are quite a few moments when Fielding is effectively satirical in his novels. Sometimes he even manages to make it work on characters we see as individuals, like Pamela, who explains to Joseph that Fanny may once have been her equal, 'but I am no longer Pamela Andrews; I am now this gentleman's lady, and, as such, I am above her. I hope I shall never behave with an unbecoming pride ...' (*Joseph Andrews,* p. 343). This is as neat a satiric barb as one could hope to find, and Fielding himself must have seen it as such. Yet, while still laughing at it as a denunciation of social climbing, one can begin to see it as a simple piece of clear-eyed characterization of Pamela. Why should the poor girl not be allowed her freshly-acquired snobbery? We are none or us perfect, and in the eighteenth century class-consciousness could be a perfectly comfortable state of mind.

With this reflection we move into the border territory between the satirical novel and the straight novel. Fielding cannot be confined to one genre or the other. What we can say is that it happens more often that reading him as satire we begin to wonder whether we are not observing a character in a novel than the other way around. Adding that he elicits a more surprised and complex sort of laughter when he defines a character than when he condemns it may amount to simply stating a personal preference. In any case it would be wrong to try and ignore his own brand of satire. More sensibly, we can argue that the satirical area in his work is narrower than it looks at first, between the territory of caricature and farce on one side and that of character-drawing on the other.

v

At this point the view of Fielding would become too confined without the admission that some of his characterization is shot through with satirical remarks. How influential we find these depends on our view of human pretensions. When Mrs Western explains to her niece, 'You are to consider me, child, as Socrates, not asking your opinion, but only informing you of mine' (*Tom Jones,* I, p. 339), this cannot escape being taken as a satirical picture of half-educated authority. When Western says about his daughter, 'If she marries the man I would ha' her, she may love whom she pleases; I shan't trouble my head about that' (*Tom Jones,* I, p. 276), it sounds too happily cynical to form part of the truth of even this unthinking character. Yet both statements belong to their natures. The line separating Fielding's satirical judgment from his character-drawing is a wavering one particularly in the theatrical dialogues that he mostly gives to the Westerns. As in the exchanges of Lady Booby with Joseph and with Mrs Slipslop, the reader is not meant to appreciate them for their subtlety. We are members of the audience, invited to enjoy the show and to feel that those who oppose the course of true love should not have their way, but should not be taken entirely seriously either.

This does not mean that the characterization in these dialogues is invariably happy-go-lucky, subject to the requirements of effective repartee only. Squire Western, although he may smell a little strong at first and takes some getting used to, is one of Fielding's durable comic characters. His way of destroying his sister's arguments as a preparation for submitting to her views, his disgust at Fellamar's bid for Sophia's hand however noble his birth, and his bawdy encouragements as soon as Tom's marrying her has become financially acceptable, are all parts of a lifelike convivial tyrant. His sister is less varied than he is, monotonously lashing out from a defensive position and apparently unaware of other opportunities, but true enough as a type and comic enough as a speaker. Most people are creatures of habit, 'and it is legitimate for any writer to picture us as such,' as Eric Bentley pointed out when refuting the idea that only unpredictable 'rounded' characters can be true to life.[10] Mrs Western's habit are firmly established, and she always says what we expect to hear from her: almost like a real human being.

The extent to which one thinks of the Westerns as satiric

10. Eric Bentley, *The Life of the Drama,* p. 41.

pictures probably corresponds to one's views of the immaculate heroes of the novels. If one sees the normal role for a human being as something like Heartfree's or Joseph's or Sophia's or Amelia's, the squire and his sister look sub-standard. If we think it is normal for us to fall short of the demands made by others and possibly also by ourselves, there is nothing unusual about them. They are personalities, somewhat louder and a good deal funnier than most.

Even if we take into account that narrative in Fielding's day was never as quiet as it became in the nineteenth century, it seems plausible to associate his particular loudness with his theatrical origins, and these origins with his gift for writing loud dialogues. There is nothing wrong with that. No compelling reason can be given why novels should be quiet and intimate rather than loud and public, and normally quiet ones may occasionally break into resoundingly public scenes; but on the whole they tend towards the intimate, with the opportunity they offer for getting inside characters, and with a solitary reader by a fireside as their audience.

Fielding was not immune to the pull of intimacy. Having started as an entertainer of theatre audiences and then become one of newspaper readers and finally of novel readers, he remained a public man to the end, but one finds intimacy gaining ground through the novels. It replaced much of the public style in *Amelia,* where the narrator no longer adresses his audience directly, there are hardly any general reflections and the main characters are a married couple instead of the conventional young lovers. In some ways the new style was imprudent and made Fielding lose more than he gained. At the same time it was incomplete, and would have worked better if he had allowed us more intimate insight into the angelic heroine herself. What one could not say is that it finished him as a comic writer. Much of the satire and the caricature disappeared, and nearly all of the artificial writing; but the more intimate sort of comedy is present, in modest quantities, and helps the shaping of character.

In the early books, comic characterization is wholly of the public sort. We form impressions of the characters; there is no question of us feeling with them. In some cases it would actually be reprehensible if we shared their feelings, whose phrasing is designed to alienate us. 'O! what a devilish thing it is,' Shamela writes to her unscrupulous mother, 'for a woman to be obliged to go to bed with a spindle-shanked young squire she doth not like, when there is a jolly parson in the same house she is fond of!' (*Shamela*, p. 336). She is only a caricature of a fictional character, and it matters little whether we are with her or not; but we do not get much closer to Abraham Adams, much as we are meant to approve of him. Only the worst of us will fail to cheer when Adams after lying still awaiting the opportunity, knocks out Fanny's ravisher; or when having had to put up with rude remarks from Peter Pounce for thinking his wealth less than £20.000 he jumps out of a moving chariot; or when having argued that no Christian should set his heart on any thing or person in this world, he suffers 'the bitterest agony' at a rumour of his son's death. All the same he remains remote from us. He is set up for our admiration, and to suggest that a funny appearance does not necessarily indicate funny principles, and can be combined with great physical strength. All his reactions are thought out by Fielding in advance, to build him up into an example; he never acquires the natural look that characters sometimes take on when their creators find that in the course of writing they have given them a richer and more varied texture than they had foreseen.

Nor does Tom Jones's character benefit from any enrichment in this sense. He is as pre-planned as Adams, and his liberties with several ladies before he is united with Sophia from part of the blueprint. Nonetheless there is at least one moment when he liberates himself and begins to look like a person in his own right rather than in Fielding's. When the Man of the Hill quotes Horace to the effect that we are best off when we are self-sufficient and not dependent on luck and cooperation: 'Here Jones smiled at some conceit which intruded itself into his imagination; but the stranger, I believe, perceived it not, and proceeded thus' (*Tom Jones*, II, p. 137). It is not surprising that the Man should ignore this smile. As a Fielding character he expects more explicit forms of self-expression, and Tom behaves as if he had no instructions from his author for this situation. That is where the novel begins to evoke intimate life. Tom is being himself, not bothering to explain that he smiles at the thought of his inability to answer Horace's requirement however impeccable its credentials.

Such moments when the characters seem to defy the narrative line and to follow the dictates of their own natures occur more easily in subsidiary parts in the novel than in the heroes and heroines, who are under constant pressure to present the author's intentions. They happen with Partridge sometimes, and with Lady Bellaston; but the most memorable sudden insights we get are with Mrs Fitzpatrick when she becomes entangled in an attempt to objectify the processes of love: 'When a husband, therefore, ceases to be the object of this passion, it is most probable some other man — I say, my dear, if your husband grows indifferent to you — if you once come to despise him — I say — that is — if you have the passion of love in you — Lud! I have bewildered myself so — but one is apt, in these abstracted considerations, to lose the concatenation of ideas, as Mr Locke says — in short, the truth is — in short, I scarce know what it is; but as I was saying, my husband returned ...' (*Tom Jones,* II, p. 279).

In such details characters convey a sense of physical presence which can remain elusive in the liveliest stretches of narrative, however enriched with ideas and descriptions. Narrative always has a point, and leads somewhere; and then suddenly life itself, which is pointless, looks through a gap in the picture. Without necessarily being very funny in isolation, such surprises provide the essence of comic liberation by relaxing the grip of sense and logic and conventional words.

Tom Jones has a few of these surprises; *Amelia* has a few more, and they stand out because there is less other comedy to distract us. The character of Miss Matthews owes its life to half a dozen liberties like the one she takes when Booth has been talking heavily about absence of dearest friends being comparable to death: 'Here Miss Matthews burst into a fit of laughter, and cried, "I sincerely ask your pardon; but I cannot help laughing at the gravity of your philosophy" ' (*Amelia,* I, p. 121). A little later she reminds one of Mrs Fitzpatrick when she gets all confused because Booth solemnly says 'I'll join with you, madam, in that,' when she said that Mandeville was wrong in denying the existence of love. ' "O, Mr Booth! In know not what I was going to say — What — Where did you leave off? — ..." ' (*Amelia,* I, p. 128).

Mrs Ellison is almost as good on a few occasions, when she says to Booth for instance that she 'would rather leave the first two syllables out of the word gentleman than the last' (*Amelia,* I, p. 238). Another of the most memorable passages of *Amelia* concerns Colonel Bath who is surprised by Booth while doing the housework for his sister who is ill, and apologizes at length for not leaving her on her own. 'I would not have you think, Mr Booth, because you have caught me in this deshabille, by coming upon me a little too abruptly — I cannot help saying a little too abruptly — that I am my sister's nurse. I know better what is due to the dignity of a man, and I have shown it in a line of battle' (*Amelia,* I, p. 145). Nearly seven feet tall and wearing a woman's bedgown, Bath begins the scene like one of Fielding's farcical figures, but turns into a living comic character when he explains himself.

There can be no safety in an assumption that Fielding would have developed this line of comedy further if he had been given the time. With his problem about how much of life is really tolerable and permissible he could not be expected to give it a free rein. We can only observe that the vein was there, more clearly visible in the later novels than before. Whenever Fielding works it one gets a closer view not only of the character but of the author, who momentarily forgets his moral preoccupations for a direct glimpse of people behaving as naturally as cats playing. He is less reliable than usual as an entertainer at such points, because he pays no attention to how many in the audience are going to enjoy or even notice his comedy; he reminds one of Tom Jones, smiling past the Man of the Hill.

vi

If one feels that Fielding's creative imagination can be more intimately observed in his character comedy than elsewhere, one might hope to approach him closer still when he talks about himself, in his introductory chapters and sometimes just in passing. This does not really happen. Part of the explanation is likely to be that while he was surprised by some of his insights into his characters, he always knew what was going to happen when he started addressing the reader about himself. Another part is that the self he presented as narrator was not the Fielding we would look for in his biography but a persona, or edition of himself designed for literary performance. One can equate this figure with Fielding the entertainer; the author masked, or dressed up, or with his face painted white, or whatever one sees as the distinctive marks of his profession. Certainly he had not turned himself into a fictional creation. He is still there behind his mask, divided in varying proportions between the man himself and the public figure.

A very finely calibrated scale would be required if we wanted to mark the exact proportions of authentic Fielding and made-up Fielding in the entertainer at different points; and it would be unlikely to reward us with greatly improved understanding. For practical purposes we can limit ourselves to defining the two extremes, and recognizing that the entertainer is never quite the author in person, nor is he ever completely somebody else.

With no reliable method at our disposal to define the real Fielding we must trust our intuition to determine that element in his role. In *The Voyage to Lisbon* (pp. 200-1; cf. above, p. 9) one might think he comes as close as anywhere to baring his soul when he talks about the sailors' jeering at him for his bad health. Nothing there allows us to think of it as a pose; but in his fiction he never sounds so much like himself — not in such direct terms. His concern to keep us entertained is always recognizable, even at moments when comedy and humour are not dominant. When he establishes the link between Sophia Western and Charlotte, his first wife who died and 'whose image can never depart from my breast' (*Tom Jones,* I, pp. 146-7), because of the 'real worth which once existed in my Charlotte' (III, p. 30), we have no reason to doubt his sincerity, but the phrases are part of the entertainment game; they have the sound of public speeches, not of confessions.

The same thing applies when he turns ironical, as he does on many of the occasions when he speaks in his own name. Good men may be a lesson to their acquaintance, he says in the first chapter of *Joseph Andrews,* but others find out about them only from books, and the people who write these 'may perhaps do a more extensive service to mankind than the person whose life originally afforded the pattern' (p. 25). This is sometimes taken seriously, although surely few statements could be more ironical particularly when applied to a work of fiction. Readers who dispute its irony are reminiscent of the student of Wayne Booth who thought that Jane Austen's Mr Bennet was serious in preferring Wickham to his other sons-in-law.[11] Perhaps their view is equally difficult to disprove, but a mirror image of Fielding's statement will be a help: people who commit crimes of violence may do less harm to mankind than those who report on them in the newspapers. Even that makes no sense, although one non-sensical element has been

11. Booth, *A Rhetoric of Irony,* p.1.

removed from Fielding's original, which concerns people writing about fictional cases of goodness. One could argue that the value of a well-written piece of fiction is obviously greater than that of an event which never occurred; but this is not really worth pointing out except as a logical joke.

However right one considers oneself on this point though, it does not take us closer to Fielding. The irony has the distancing effect that George R. Levine talks about: 'It becomes an invisible barrier — or, more properly, perhaps, a reversed telescope — that is placed between the object and both the sympathy and empathy of the reader.'[12] In *Joseph Andrews* the experience of distancing is even more pronounced when Fielding writes his 'sarcastical pane-gyric' on vanity and explains that he does this 'for no other purpose than to lengthen out a short chapter' (p. 83). Very possibly this was true enough, but it has nothing confidential about it.

There is a more personal and intimate quality about the sentence that opens Book V of *Tom Jones:* 'Peradventure there may be no parts in this prodigious work which will give the reader less pleasure in the perusing than those which have given the author the greatest pains in composing' (I, p. 205). This is indeed perfectly possible, as many authors of works prodigious and otherwise have been aware. It is also nicely phrased, and for a moment or two one may think the author and ourselves are going to be intimate after all; but when he goes on he calls himself 'we' as he does at times, and the illusion is soon dispersed.

Sometimes Fielding manages to maintain his distance while at the same time putting up a persuasive show of throwing reserve to the winds, as when he quotes Horace on the need for authors themselves to weep before they can make readers do so, and continues, 'I am convinced I never make my reader laugh heartily but where I have laughed before him; unless it should happen at any time that instead of laughing with me he should be inclined to laugh at me' (*Tom Jones,* II, p. 160). Without any suggestion why he thinks we might want to laugh at him, this modesty fails to bring us together.

Whether closer to us or remoter from us, and however credibly true to his experience, Fielding preserves his invisible barrier. At times when the irony becomes extreme it seems he might create a

12. Levine, *Henry Fielding and the Dry Mock,* p. 88.

wholly fictional narrator, talking unconcernedly about 'a foolish zeal for a certain ridiculous imaginary thing called liberty, to which great men are observed to have a great animosity' (*Jonathan Wild*, p. 149). This impression never gets time to settle down; the author is always there to prevent misunderstandings, which as he was well aware irony causes easily.

So Fielding keeps his narrator suspended at different points between reality and fiction; never quite coinciding with himself, in jest or in earnest. We are rarely given time to forget him for more than a few minutes' reading. 'In which, after some very fine writing, the history goes on,' he heads a chapter (*Joseph Andrews*, p. 47). 'It would be impertinent to insert a discourse which chiefly turned on the relation of matters already well known to the reader' (*Joseph Andrews*, p. 77); 'I shall refer it to my reader to make what observations he pleases on this incident' (*Joseph Andrews*, p. 196); 'And here I strictly forbid all male critics to intermeddle with a circumstance which I have recounted only for the sake of the ladies, and upon which they only are at liberty to comment' (*Tom Jones*, I, p. 296); 'some readers may perhaps be pleased with these minute circumstances ...; and others, to whom they may appear trivial, will, we hope, at least pardon them' (*Tom Jones*, III, p. 253).

This sort of thing goes on all the time until we come to *Amelia*, in whose subdued narrative atmosphere, although we can hear the narrator clearly enough, exuberant displays of generalization and over-statement and self-disparagement and deference to the reader have no place. Naturally *Amelia* sounds monotonous by comparison, with its sad little voice recounting what the hostess 'cries' to the visitor and what the visitor cries in return. In compensation we may have a more intimate view of Fielding himself, but the complaint has always been that he was much more fun before. To the casual reader it may even have appeared as if he did not take himself altogether seriously at such moments as when, in the sixteenth introductory chapter of *Tom Jones*, he suggests that the point of these introductions, as of prologues in the theatre, is that they allow us to practice our hissing, to get our bile up for criticizing the rest, and to think of other things (III, p. 199).

In the end it turns out that he was perfectly serious all the time in his views on relations and human qualities and emotions. It was only story-telling he had his doubts about. Argue as he might in favour of the comic epic-poem in prose and the new province of writing in which he was the legislator, something dubious continued to cling to the practice of presenting one's moral philosophy in the form of made-up stories. By the time George Eliot and Henry James wrote their works there was wide agreement on the immense importance to civilization of the experiences of imaginary persons. This was not so in Fielding's days, and although he came to the subject with fresh views of his own, he does not sound unwaveringly sure of the validity of his new writing with its slender classical foundation in *Don Quixote* and one lost work by Homer.

The narrator as entertainer was a great help. He could supply the link between the classically-based view of human nature and the frivolous freshness of the genre in which it was displayed. The former he interpreted by turning himself nearly into Fielding, believing in values adopted only after profound thought; for the latter he became the friend of his audience, telling them about the wonderful type of story he was developing for them, putting them at ease by mocking his own pretensions and ridiculing those of others, and constantly concerned to eliminate the danger of boredom.

If one says that Fielding attached importance to his views of human nature but not a great deal to his stories, confirmation can be found in his endings. Calling his works histories in contrast to the romances that were the traditional form of fiction, he was not trying to suggest that there was a factual basis for the events narrated but referring to his view of human life and experience. Without pretending that he invariably manages to maintain the strictest realism in his psychological and social observations, we must admit that realism is never completely ignored — never, that is, until the last few chapters of his novels. The Heartfrees, the Andrewses who become the Wilsons, the Joneses and the Booths all end happily not because they overcome their difficulties or even because they are lucky, but because they are snatched away out of reality by a magic hand.

It is possible to justify these happy endings in two ways. They can be related to the epic tradition that Fielding was adapting in a way of his own; the Reversal of Fortune was a familiar device in that genre.[13] More personally, they would suit him by suggesting,

---

13. See e.g. John Butt, *Oxford History of English Literature,* Vol. VIII, *The Mid-Eighteenth Century* (Oxford, 1979), p. 414.

as the royal interventions did at the end of Molière plays, that such happiness was not likely to occur in the real world. The type of historical truthfulness that he practised had limited use for verisimilitude of events, and would have found no inspiration in the mock authenticity of Defoe or the pseudo-mock authenticity of Swift. All that mattered was the accuracy of the insight and the judgment of human behaviour. Stories that sounded or felt like real truth would be more likely to confuse than to help the reader's appreciation of those qualities. Important though narrative might be for the literary form of one's work, it could not be allowed a decisive share in its meaning. It provided a framework for one's ideas. It had no need to convey any of them.

Ascribing to Fielding a lack of seriousness about his storytelling does not imply that he would have tolerated the laughter of critics and other 'reptiles' about it. Entertainers, however delightfully self-depreciatory, easily become vicious when not adequately admired, and Fielding had a lifelong quarrel with 'snarlers in the republic of letters,'[14] and tended to feel that the best critic was a dead and distant critic.[15] Fortunately his story-telling has been admired as much as his other qualities by many critics and historians. Moreover, the idea that he was not entirely serious about his narrative is not used as adverse criticism even here. It helps recognition of the range of variations through which the personality of the narrator moved in his novels. Also it enables us to see that while at first Fielding seems to be ironical about himself in some of his comments, the irony is more specifically aimed at one experimental section of his writing, and does not commit his own personality. In fact, when we find him being ironical about what looks like himself we move away from the intimacy in which some of his character-comedy had involved us. Before long, if we had pressed him, he would have evaded us in purely verbal humour again, thus closing the circle of this argument.

Clearly, Fielding's novels will not be properly understood by a

14. *Jacobite's Journal* no. 8, January 23, 1748, quoted in Ioan Williams (ed.), *The Criticism of Henry Fielding*, p. 208.

15. '... I can never be understood ... to insinuate that there are no proper judges of writing ... Such were Aristotle, Horace and Longinus among the ancients, Dacier and Bossu among the French, and some perhaps among us ...' (*Tom Jones*, II, p. 244).

reader who is insensitive to their humour. One can also agree with Battestin that humour is the most memorable thing about them. When it comes to calling it 'the warm breath ... that animates his fiction,' however, our ways may have to part. The animation comes from somewhere else.

III THE FORMALIST

i

'If it cannot be put into a phrase it is no subject for a novel,' said Percy Lubbock; however complex the book in its final form, its essence should be 'expressible in ten words that reveal its unity.'[1] By that firm old standard, Fielding's novels are faultless; although one might chafe at the limitation of ten words, there can be no difficulty about getting the subjects into single phrases. We know what these stories are about, and what the author is trying to say in them; no ambiguities disturb our recollection of their outlines. In their basic design they are the clearest of novels to remember, and it is mostly these designs that stay in the mind. It can be disconcerting to find that much of their detail is quickly forgotten. A few characterizations and some scraps of incident will cling to the outline, but most of them are smoothly absorbed in a general idea of the book and leave no mark of their own.

Except perhaps in the case of very systematic readers this is not customary with novels. More often, one's first memories are of individual characters and incidents, and a further effort is required to bring back the framework of the story. Doubtless their authors had something to say, but the world is full of people who have things to say and it is impossible to remember much of them. When they create images and incidents it is another matter; these are added to the remains of our own experience of life, and although for most of us they are different because unlived, some of them prove just as memorable.

If Fielding's individual characters and incidents offer little resistance to oblivion this can be related to his expressed preference for generalization. As an epic-poet-in-prose, he was not a novelist of the sort who feel that the truth of human experience is to be derived from observation of every incident in its own right. His dominant idea on this point was that individual cases cannot

1. Percy Lubbock, *The Craft of Fiction,* pp. 41-2.

help bearing out general rules. This is a notion we could hardly do without, unless we gave up generalizing altogether. At the same time we have to cope with the contrasting notion that experience tends to be more complicated than the rules, and to confute or damage them. Various balances have been struck between these two ideas by different authors. Looking back on Fielding two-and-a-half centuries later, it is one of his most obvious characteristics that he sides with the general view in preference to the specific more insistently than any later novelist who is still read.

His motivation and justification would have to be found in the epic tradition that he invoked; but his continuation of it was never quite thorough enough. E.M.W. Tillyard has argued that Tom Jones, who came closest to being an epic hero, cannot be said to 'turn into a symbolic figure, an Everyman, as Crusoe does. He remains a likable and adequate comic hero.'[2] In these terms, Tom Jones was a generalized figure who failed to achieve epic dimensions. Fortunately, Fielding did not restrict him to his 'adequate comic' role. He did respond to the call of the unique and unruly individual incident on some occasions. His characterization of Adams offers a few early examples, as does the love life of Tom Jones. He would not have regarded close observation as a first requirement for the novelist, but it looks as if he gradually acquired the taste.

Unique incidents may be taken to appeal more immediately to the modern reader. This is not to say that illustrations of a general theory of human behaviour are only a primitive form, or that they have lost all their power. We tend to deplore their unevocative formality and recognize little more in them than old-world charm; but it should be possible to show them in such a way that more of their original colour becomes apparent.

Pictorial description is not the only form they occur in, but it is logically the best one to discuss first.

ii

On arriving at Tyburn, Jonathan Wild has a last fling as a professional criminal. The narrator includes this in his story of the life 'as it serves to show the most admirable conservation of character in our hero to the last moment, ... that, whilst the

2. E.M.W. Tillyard, *The Epic Strain in the English Novel,* p. 58.

ordinary was busy in his ejaculations, Wild, in the midst of the shower of stones, &c., which played upon him, applied his hands to the parson's pocket, and emptied it of his bottle-screw, which he carried out of the world in his hand' (*Jonathan Wild,* p. 200). It is a delightful touch, confirming Wild's crookedness and at the same time exonerating him, because he is obviously inspired by a motive beyond greed, but there is no attempt to show us Wild in action. The description is only a report on what he did, compounding its casualness about detail with the awkward clash of its two references to the hero's hand. The scene would have been funnier and more disturbing if we had been offered a glimpse of Wild practising his art, bringing out his resemblance to a child playing, unaware of the lethal world around it.

If one were to see this as one of Fielding's missed chances, it has to be taken into account that here more than in his later works of fiction he was anxious to make his point, which is about people's misguided conception of heroism. Nowhere in *Jonathan Wild* is there any directly observed detail. The story exists to confirm a theoretical view, and although pedantic it is not a baseless distinction that often leads to its being left out of a discussion of Fielding's novels. It reminds one, not in its subject but in its treatment, of the romances based on French examples that dominated the fiction market at the time.[3]

This is not to the same extent true of *Joseph Andrews,* a less urgent book whose basic tension results not from the alternatives of crime and goodness but of fulfilment and disappointment. Parts of the story are told, and some of the narrator's views presented, with a relaxed air of casual talk which Fielding would never have allowed himself side by side with the heavy irony in his treatment of crime. A scene like the one where Adams fails to notice the bridge and wades through the stream would be as lost in *Jonathan Wild* as the picture of Lady Booby and Pamela who 'fixed their eyes on two looking-glasses' and paid 'a cross compliment' to each other's charm in comparison to Fanny's (*Joseph Andrews,* pp. 110 and 333).

In *Joseph Andrews* these two scenes belong to a small number which come close to suggesting direct observation and a readiness on the part of the author to allow incidents to occur independently

3. See for instance William H.McBurney, *Four before Richardson.*

of general laws. At the opposite end of the scale, as narratives rigidly dominated by their moral purpose, can be set the digressions: the stories of Leonora and Bellarmine, of Mr Wilson, and of Leonard and Paul, which are as far out of reach of individual observation as anything in *Jonathan Wild.*

Whatever Fielding himself and his contemporaries may have found in the digressions, for us their best use is as an immediately available standard of comparison against which to judge the relative measure of natural life in other scenes. When Leonora first realized that Bellarmine showed an interest in her,

> there was nothing so foolish as her behaviour: she played a thousand childish tricks, distorted her person into several shapes, and her face into several laughs, without any reason. In a word, her carriage was as absurd as her desires, which were to affect an insensibility of the stranger's admiration, and at the same time a triumph, from that admiration, over every woman in the room (*Joseph Andrews,* p. 126).

This is a perfect example of descriptions at the mercy of dislike, and incapable of evoking a girl with a shape of her own. On the fringes of Mr Wilson's story we find his garden praised in:

> No parterres, no fountains, no statues embellished this little garden. Its only ornament was a short walk, shaded on each side by a filbert hedge, with a small alcove at one end, whither in hot weather the gentleman and his wife used to retire and divert themselves with their children, who played in the walk before them (*Joseph Andrews,* pp. 255-6).

Compared to that tableau of abstract domestic happiness almost anything in the novel proper will seem vivid and colourful, but Leonora is not always far away. Beau Didapper was 'no hater of women, for he always dangled after them; yet so little subject to lust, that he had, among those who knew him best, the character of great moderation in his pleasures' (p. 356). Nor does 'the red liquor which his veins contained, and the white liquor which the pot contained, ran in one stream down his face and clothes' (p. 292) suggest attentive observation when one realizes that the liquor distinguished by its whiteness is meant to be urine.

However, the visual elements of Joseph Andrews often reveal a measure of original observation, not as dominant as in the wading scene but more effective than in the pub fight. The return to the reality of the novel after the Wilson story is signalled by the death of the spaniel puppy who has been shot by the local squire's son and 'came limping in all bloody and laid himself at his mistress's feet' (p. 258). If that has an extraordinary quality it is as a narrative twist rather than as an example of visualization, but the scene is straightforward and conveys a stronger concern for the dog than was spent on Leonora or on Wilson himself.

One of the signs of relaxation in *Joseph Andrews* is the ability of the narrator to take his task lightly at times. Joseph's 'air which, to those who have not seen many noblemen, would give an idea of nobility' (p. 48) is not strictly speaking a piece of visualization, but with its slightly snobbish irony it does encourage the reader to imagine things for himself and enjoy the freedom of a world where there are at least some scenes that may be prized for their own sake.

Joseph Andrews offers far more variety of mood and judgment than *Jonathan Wild*. Still, it is not memorable for its individual detail, as novels go. One has to put in extra work to get the events clearly ranged in one's mind; and the same thing goes for *Tom Jones*. There it is not only the view of human nature in general which dominates the details of behaviour, it is also the plot. *Joseph Andrews* has a happy-go-lucky shape compared to the celebrated tripartite structure of the later book; at the same time Fielding was even more specific in defining the moral qualities that belonged to his idea of a good man.

Not that he neglected his details. On the contrary, he was if anything more attentive to them, but they had to serve the cause of the structure and they are usually so stylized that one is not likely to give them any significance of their own. An arbitrary element will be impossible to avoid in any particular comparison to illustrate this general point, but at least a partial confirmation can be derived from looking at the death of the little dog mentioned above side by side with that of Sophia's little bird released by Blifil. It is a charming idea to blame the bird perching on a branch nearby for 'forgetting all the favours it had received from Sophia,' but Tom strikes one as lacking sense to an excessive degree when he climbs the tree as if he was trying to retrieve a cat. He falls into the canal, the bird is killed by a hawk, Blifil gives a sanctimonious account of the event to Mr Allworthy, and Sophia bursts into tears: everything falls neatly into place in the appointed plan of the novel, but nothing in the description of the incident brings to mind a scene with real people and a genuine bird (I, pp. 150-2).

Much the same can be said of a scene whose first half is intended to have a dual visual impact, on the reader but also on three of the four card-players taking part in it, when Tom Edwards reports the rumour of Tom Jones's death and Sophia tries to continue dealing as she had just begun to do but

> having dealt three cards to one, and seven to another, and ten to a third, at last dropped the rest from her hand, and fell back in her chair. — The company behaved as usual on these occasions. The usual disturbance ensued, the usual assistance was summoned, and Sophia at last, as it is usual, returned again to life, and was soon after, at her earnest desire, led to her own apartment; ... (III, P. 150).

It is hard to imagine a description more literally generalized than that, and although all the 'usuals' can be recognized as aids to a light-hearted view of the incident, they insist too heavily. Such Fielding scenes one tends to read several times thinking something must have escaped attention; they have so little centre.

Whenever one begins to think that all the author ever wanted of his scenes was that they should subordinate themselves to the plan, occasions come to mind when they do more. Sometimes in *Tom Jones* this is achieved casually, without much visual concentration, as when Mrs Waters, topless after her struggle with Northerton, refuses Tom's offer of his coat and follows him to Upton through the fields while he keeps his eyes decently turned away, except on the many occasions when she stumbles or has to be helped over stiles (II, p. 499).

At other times visual effects occur that do have the power to make impressions of their own. When Sophia returns to Lady Bellaston's house from the theatre, she enters a room which she thinks empty and walks over to the looking-glass; but Tom is there, motionless as a statue, and she sees first his reflection and then, 'instantly turning about, she perceived the reality of the vision: upon which she gave a violent scream, and scarce preserved herself from fainting till Jones was able to move to her and support her in his arms.' This is vivid, far from the faceless world of the Leonoras, until Fielding concludes lamely with: 'To paint the looks or thoughts of either of these lovers is beyond my power' (III, p. 81).

The generalizing unspecific tendency remains the dominant one, and quickly resumes its sway after occasional intensely visualized moments. When Tom has been told to leave Allworthy's house forever he sits down by the side of a brook and 'presently fell into the most violent agonies, tearing his hair from his head, and using most other actions which generally accompany fits of madness, rage and despair' (I, p. 318). When Sophia enters the room at Upton Partridge retreats to a corner, 'struck with the utmost awe and astonishment at the splendor of the lady's dress. Indeed she had a much better title to respect than this; for she was one of the most beautiful creatures in the world' (II, p. 206). When Allworthy has recognized Blifil's crookedness and embraces Tom, 'Mrs Miller entering the room at that moment, after a gentle rap which was not perceived, and seeing Jones in the arms of his uncle, the poor woman in an agony of joy fell upon her knees, and burst forth into the most ecstatic thanksgivings to heaven for what had happened' (III, p. 354). When Tom gets up in the night after he has been struck by Northerton's bottle and the sentry sees him approaching, white-faced and with a blood-stained bandage round his head, with a sword in one hand and a candle in the other, 'his hair began gently to lift up his grenadier cap; and in the same instant his knees fell to blows with each other' (II, p. 50).

The last-quoted instance is perhaps the most telling of all, but what can be said of it applies to the preceding ones as well: these are not descriptions of an imagined reality, but of imagined drawings and engravings, straight ones in some cases and caricatures in others. It will be difficult at all times to know what exactly any particular author sees in his own imagination before he sets out to describe a scene, but this does not matter so much as that it should look as if he had seen human beings. With some authors one becomes over-conscious of the words on the page and sees reality in the form of a printed text; with others one has moments when the imagined reality becomes so vivid that the words can no longer contain it and one has to look up. Between those two extremes there is room for the innumerable compromises that novel-reading requires, and the reader always finds himself between two worlds.

What is different in the case of Fielding is that the imagined reality quite often is not that of life itself. Many of his pictured scenes do their work better when one thinks of them as related to prints. They suggest the over-emphasis that is required when natural movement is missing from a scene. Some of the pictures evoked, such as that of Mrs Miller entering the room and seeing the reconciliation, look as if they were conceived as engravings in black and white from the first moment; and the idea that readers were supposed to recognize those sorts of scenes from their collections of prints is supported by Fielding's frequent trick of leaving the description unfinished, adding sometimes that we all know such situations and if we do not there is little he can do for us.[4]

His partiality for print-like visual scenes can be variously explained by a need for more emphatic and expressive outward behaviour than sober description can be relied on to provide; by a liking for the originals coupled with an assumption that his readers would find them easy and congenial; and by a wish to charge his scenes with extra significance by means of traditional signs and symbols. That he should have experienced a practical need for added expression sounds plausible enough in theory, because of the small amount of information about his characters' inner life that his style of narrative provided. When Tom is on his own and we want to know what he feels it is a help when he acts it out, tearing his hair from his head for instance. Such formal action can also come in useful at times to cut down or even eliminate complex stretches of dialogue. When Blifil is unmasked, he 'asked pardon of his brother in the most vehement manner, prostrated himself on the ground, and kissed his feet ... Jones could not so far check his disdain, but that it a little discovered itself in his countenance at this extreme servility' (*Tom Jones,* III, p. 357). On the other hand, when the soldier's hair stands up and slowly lifts his cap, this makes good farcical comedy, but the scene could have turned out more effective because more true with realistic means. Nor was there any need for Partridge to retreat to the other end of the room

4. Collections of prints may not have been as common in the 1740's as they were later in the century (see Dorothy George, *Hogarth to Cruik-shank,* p. 17), but the print industry and the public's response were well under way, particularly after the passing in May 1735 of the Engravers' Act, inspired by Hogarth, which ensured the exclusive rights of designers and engravers for a period of 14 years (see Ronald Paulson, *Hogarth,* I, pp. 359-363).

when Sophia entered; again, his over-reaction demands laughter without bothering to amuse us. In such cases it looks as if Fielding simply took the easiest way.

It seems unlikely that more than a minority of the pictorial scenes will make more sense if we interpret all the possible symbolic signs. The existence of the signs is not in doubt. Martin Battestin has written convincingly about them in *The Providence of Wit*; P.J. de Voogd has gone further into some of them in *Henry Fielding and William Hogarth*. Only a rash opponent would try to dispute that as Joseph Andrews represented chastity, so Tom Jones stood for prudence, or at least prudence in the making, and Sophia for wisdom, and that the mirror we see Sophia looking in may have a symbolic significance, as do Allworthy's estate and the view from Mazard Hill.[5] Continuing in this direction, one may also accept that Sophia's little bird released by Blifil represents her chastity, threatened by the unwanted suitor.[6]

The explanations are only partial, though. It can be assumed that Fielding was acquainted with at least some traditional emblematic imagery, and that he would enjoy making use of it in his print-like scenes. One would not expect him to be particularly wary of introducing such elements into a novel like *Tom Jones* several of whose components, such as its structure and characters like Thwackum and Square and Blifil, were abstractions anyway.

After the admissions come the reservations and contradictions. If Sophia's bird stands for her chastity and Blifil is the evil character threatening it, not only is this a superfluous comment on a relationship that would be clear to the reader without it, it also twists the situation into a shape somewhat at odds with the other evidence. What Blifil threatens is Sophia's freedom of choice rather than her chastity; he wants her money, not her body. Trying to think what deeper meaning could be implied when Tom in his attempt to retrieve the bird falls into the water, one feels increasingly at a loss. Surely one could not argue that this would be Fielding's considered way to clarify or reinforce his narrative? It looks rather as if he might have had a recollection that little caged birds meant chastity, and decided that it would be in order for a nature like Blifil's to be nasty to it.

5. Martin C. Battestin, *The Providence of Wit*, pp. 183-9.
6. P.J. De Voogd, *Henry Fielding and William Hogarth*, p. 112.

When Sophia looks in the mirror and sees Tom standing behind her, it is doubtless legitimate to recall the mirror's symbolic association with both vanity and the contemplative life; but it would be a waste of a memorable scene to regard it only in those terms and overlook its merits as a piece of novel-writing. De Voogd describes the way Sophia looks round ('... instantly turning about ...') as 'curiously formal', and he finds the idea of Tom standing like a statue lacking in reality.[7] There is plenty of room for disagreement here; both the instant turn and the statue seem unusually real and true for Fielding.

If such scenes are treated as extensions of the mixed style that he was often condemned for in his own day, they look their best. Not that the mixed style was supposed to be two different ones simultaneously; that is why these two cases should be called extensions rather than just examples. They fit in with the idea that Fielding was a writer of fiction feeling his way towards a form for the novel of moral and social criticism, yet remaining attached to the older ways.

In any case it is worth seeing his pictorial scenes as close relations to those of contemporary artists, primarily of Hogarth whom he mentions and praises at numerous points in his work, and whom he refers to as 'my friend.' This friendship is a puzzling matter, because there is no other evidence of it than Fielding's refer-ences in his books and some drawings that Hogarth did for him, and the one he did of him. Surely de Voogd is right in finding it strange that after Fielding's death Hogarth, who was famous for his visual memory, could not do a portrait of him until Margaret Collier had come up with a silhouette. How close or detached or casual was their friendship?

We have no special business to be asking this question in the present context, except that it suggests the possibility of a virtually non-existent relationship coupled with a strong sense of being on the same side in the artistic conflicts of the time. This would not diminish the value of the protestations of friendship, which on the contrary sound more authentic in reference to professional than to private relations. There was always an influence passing between them, says Ronald Paulson, running mostly from Hogarth to Fielding up to 1742, and then in the opposite direction, tending

7. ibid. p. 111.

perhaps to make Hogarth 'more self-conscious and defensive, more verbal and polemical.'[8] This makes sense even if one takes into account that Fielding's most pictorial novel appeared seven years after the reversal of the influence. Having used Hogarth to strengthen his confidence in morally expressive pictorial scenes he no longer needed him as a master once he had found his feet as a novelist. He was largely different from him in his view of the moral nature of man, and of the importance of satire, being more given to life-enhancing or at least to the encouragement of virtue. In the end he even forgot the early lessons, and in *Amelia* denied himself and the reader most of the pictorial pleasure that had been a major component of *Tom Jones.*

Paulson would probably not be inclined to assent to this, with his opinion that Richardson's scenes were worked out in visual terms 'more than any other scenes before Sterne's, certainly more than Fielding's.'[9] Against the background of that general judgment, *Amelia* does not provide much of a contrast with its predecessors. We will have to agree nonetheless that it is remarkably devoid of visual components. The eye is allowed to rest, or to roam. No more travels between London and the West Country, no inns and chamberpot fights, no horses or crossroads; nor for that matter any characters gazing or sighing or struggling or fainting or revealing their natures and moods by how they unmistakably look. These people no sooner catch sight of each other than they start talking; when they have finished they go their different ways in hardly specified streets of London.

There are a few exceptions. When Booth enters the room and finds Atkinson on his knees before his wife who seems to be furious, and Amelia who is also present bursts into tears, one is reminded of the old days of *Tom Jones* (*Amelia,* II, pp. 231-2). There is also a remarkable visual effect built into the narrative, starting with the mysterious visitor to the Booth household in the absence of the family; more than a hundred pages later he turns out to have been Dr Harrison who was so unfavourably impressed by the expensive presents from a certain noble Lord he saw that little else was needed to make him decide to have Booth arrested once again for his debts (*Amelia,* II, p. 122).

8. Paulson, *Hogarth,* I, pp. 468-71.
9. Paulson, *Hogarth,* II, p. 11.

There used to be scores of such descriptive effects; now there are only two or three. 'O, Shakespeare! had I thy pen! O, Hogarth! had I thy pencil!' Fielding had exclaimed in *Tom Jones* (II, p. 229). He could imagine using either in those days; this was no longer true by the time of *Amelia*. Hogarth and the pictures and prints are left behind. One could interpret this as a sign of sadness and seriousness, assuming that the pictorial writing had been fun for Fielding but the real business of life was too earnest. At the same time one could revert to the point about the increasing ambiguity in Fielding's moral judgment, and suggest that he found the old word-pictures too blatant and positivist for his new purpose. The two interpretations need not exclude each other. In any case it is clear that we see less of the characters than we used to do, and we hear more. Those of us who think that the ambiguity of judgment results in a more lifelike account of human relations might be tempted to see the stylistic development also going in the direction of greater naturalness; but the dialogue we hear in *Amelia* could not be described as natural without qualifications and distinctions.

iii

Fielding's character not only pose visually; they also pose in dialogue when required, expressing themselves in such formal or artificial or extravagant terms that hardly any resemblance to life outside literature remains. Once again, they are far from consistent. They address each other in more different ways than the characters of other novelists, ranging from the oratorical, by way of various kinds of comic or emotional exaggeration and some forms of the simply factual to an intimately natural vein.

The definition of naturalness is always elusive, as students of the eighteenth century which made much use of the concept are the first to know. Novel dialogues, although they can sound relatively unaffected, will never get away from artificiality, even in our age which has isolated 'an ear for dialogue' as a praiseworthy quality in a novelist. Only at privileged moments will they achieve a deceptive imitation of the way people speak. Living speech mechanically recorded looks too much of a mess, logically and grammatically, to be tolerable in writing, and although the rhythm of a single person's words can occasionally be captured there is no hope of reproducing that of a discussion of two or more. With this point in mind, one could argue as strongly in favour of an intentionally artificial dialogue as of one that struggles to appear lifelike. What one would still require even in artificial dialogue is that a character's speech should be adapted to his personality and not just consist of formal rhetoric. An inability to differentiate between ways of speaking is one of the weaknesses of the romances that preceded the rise of novel, and is what makes them so unmemorable.

In the oratorical forms of Fielding's dialogue cases of individual and generalized expression both occur. Adams varies from the almost intimate to the grandly ecclesiastical but manages to remain in character with the assistance of his calling, which demands an elevated tone at times. This cannot be said of Allworthy; when he explains to Jenny why it is wrong to have an illegitimate child, or to Tom how important it is to act with prudence, there is nothing in his words that helps to recognize him as an individual. Amelia is too soft and modest a girl to go in for sermons like those of Allworthy; but most of what she says sounds quite impersonal, except that it testifies to exceptional purity of feeling and freedom from second thoughts. Jonathan Wild, surprisingly, has moments when his rhetoric is rather more arresting than that of some of the later characters. The monologue which he ends by telling himself that instead of being sorry for ruining an innocent man he ought 'rather to weep with Alexander that I have ruined no more than to regret the little I have done,' although far removed from any conceivable criminal idiom, could hardly come from anyone else (*Jonathan Wild,* p. 159). Tom Jones, when he criticizes Nightingale for his intention to leave Nancy Miller, succeeds in being intimate and stuffy in the same sentence ('Lookee, Mr Nightingale,' said Jones, 'I am no canting hypocrite ...,' — see above, p. 8).

As usual when Fielding loses touch with the realities of everyday dialogue, the latter part of that statement contains a moral precept which he offers to the reader as a truth not dependent on which character happens to say it. The sentiments he voices at such moments are excellent, not in the sense that one invariably agrees with them but that they are meant to define a standard of conduct free from considerations of self-interest and convenience. They contribute nothing to the novel: they make blank spaces in the characters because they sound untrue to life and in the end leave characters such as Allworthy who hardly ever talk in any other way wholly indistinct.

It is certainly not as if Fielding showed himself indifferent to the real sound of dialogue. On two occasions in *Joseph Andrews* he is almost scientific in his pursuit of realism: when he tries to reproduce an exchange without narrative significance but full of slang terms between a young fellow and a coachman[10], and when he strengthens Beau Didapper's incredibly rude but apparently not unforgivable remark to Lady Booby about her face with a footnote: 'Lest this should appear unnatural to some readers, we think proper to acquaint them that it is taken verbatim from very polite conversation' (*Joseph Andrews,* p. 357).

Joseph Andrews has more of those isolated bits of lifelike dialogue than *Tom Jones.* Lady Bellaston produces a few gems, and so do Partridge and Honour and Mrs Western. On the whole the later book is less notable for its occasional felicities of dialogue than for the development of the comic spate of words. The form is familiar from *Joseph Andrews,* and could have served well in *Jonathan Wild* where Tishy Snap would have practised it with gusto but does not get a chance. Lady Booby and Mrs Slipslop are its earliest virtuoso performers, producing an effect that reminds Fielding connoisseurs of his beginnings in the theatre, built up as it is out of rapid revuelike repartee. Do as I bid you, says Lady Booby to Slipslop, 'and don't shock my ears with your beastly language,' to which the gentlewoman-in-waiting replies without hesitation that 'people's ears are sometimes the nicest part about them' (*Joseph Andrews,* p. 53).

A direct line leads from this dispute to the quarrels of Squire Western and his sister, and to the dialogue between Sophia and Mrs Honour on the eve of their flight, when Sophia suggests that a pistol would be the normal way to protect one's virtue, and the maid replies that, to be sure, 'one's virtue is a dear thing, especially to us poor servants; for it is our livelihood, as a body may say; yet I mortally hate fire-arms, for so many accidents happen by them' (*Tom Jones,* I, p. 362).

The quality of Mrs Waters' language is not inferior to this, when

---

10. *Joseph Andrews,* p. 88: ' "You be hanged," says the other; "for five guineas you shall shoot at my a —." "Done," says the coachman; "I'll pepper you better than ever you was peppered by Jenny Bouncer." '

she counters the offer of a gown from a inn-keeper's wife with a blistering refusal ending in 'I would have you know, creature, I have a spirit above that' (*Tom Jones,* II, p. 173). One could not say that such surprises strengthen the narrative or the characterization of the novels; but they enliven the general impression, by providing light but potentially far-reaching relief. Partridge makes a valuable contribution to it when he counters Tom's recommendation of death for a good cause with 'What are all the ringing of bells, and bonfires, to one that is six foot under ground? there will be an end of poor Partridge' (*Tom Jones,* II, p. 312). Characters who say such things are clearly beings of a lower order than Adams and Joseph and Tom and Allworthy; yet most if not all readers have a vein running through their natures that is more concerned about their poor selves than about the excellence of their death; and so, one may suppose, did Fielding. There is a measure of comic exaggeration in these scenes, but more than the oratorical exaggerations which point to moral qualities and obligations, they deal with human truth.

Amelia has no major examples of this comic technique. The significance of its absence may be most justly seen if one interprets it as not merely a decline in Fielding's exuberance, but a loss of confidence and enjoyment in the reproduction of forms of speech. There is a parallel here with the loss of enjoyment of pictorial description, and both are symptoms of a general detachment from novel-writing as the playing of a game, which becomes most dominantly apparent in the looser structure of *Amelia* compared to the earlier novels. This is a subject in itself; in the meantime one can observe it in the details of dialogue as much as of visual description, and gather further material for a judgment on whether all this is mostly a matter of loss and decline and too little enjoyment or of a new seriousness.

If one says that there is more balance in the moral view of characters like Miss Matthews and Colonel James than of Lady Bellaston and Blifil this does not mean that Fielding is willing to condone their faults. The punishments meted out at the end of *Amelia* show differently. It is not that the faults have become venial; it is that the carriers of them are recognized as normal people instead of miscreants with protruding eyes, flat breasts and manners either coarse or unctuous.

This has to come out in the way they talk, inevitably because they are revealed to us by hardly anything else; and although the dialogue of *Amelia* has points in common with that of the earlier books, the overall impression it leaves is quite different. The earlier form belongs to a world of superlatives and exclamation marks and astonishment at people's extraordinary behaviour. Every encounter becomes a celebration of a delightful or objectionable extraordinariness. With Wild, the monster criminal, this could not be otherwise. It looks less inevitable in the case of Adams, who displays Fielding's first attempts at balanced characterization. In spite of the faults that temper his goodness and that make him more of a fellow-man than a model of moral excellence, it is only in scenes dominated by other people's astonishing behaviour that he takes on a passing resemblance to an ordinary human being, as in his subdued mood after the outrageous conduct of the squire and his friend in Book III. Normally whenever he takes part in the story he is the one to keep us surprised, whether by rolling downhil in the dark or flinging his Aeschylus in the fire, holding forth on the comparative merits of public and private schools or showing himself unfamiliar with the ways of the world. Even when in the long run some of his actions and pronouncements are in accordance with what one has come to expect of him, his idiosyncrasies are the elements in his performance that are stressed. The ideal Fielding reader, one often feels, would be one who did not chuckle and contemplate, but jumped about in his chair and shouted.

The same exuberance and expectation of an exuberant response mark *Tom Jones*. It is not just wicked souls like Blifil, or small-time crooks like Black George, or domestic tyrants like Mrs Western or images of moral perfection like Mr Allworthy who are meant to surprise us; the very philosophers, not only in their personalities but in their ideas, contribute to life's fund of oddities and colourful contrasts. Squire Western, with his merciless devotion to his daughter's interest, is only the most extravagant of all these characters. Not content with his extraordinary conduct and views, Fielding even devised a form of phonetic spelling to convey his Somerset accent. He never did this for another character, and it seems expressive of the gusto with which he went about the business of making a book out of the amazing materials of his invention.

In *Amelia* there is nothing left of this. The characters' speech is no longer designed to amaze and upset and delight us; they talk as they do because that is the sort of characters they are, even Amelia herself and her husband. Although as models of love and goodness they have much in common with the loving couples who preceded them, their married state makes them look more like people caught in the toils of life than like heralds of a new promise. Tom losing his money evokes the image of a dangerous world excitingly open, Booth losing his brings to mind his hungry children, and Amelia leaning on a table. Also the Booths inevitably feel the effect of the other characters in the book. We are no longer in a world where the extraordinariness of people's behaviour is to be seen as stimulating, which is by no means purely loss. Instead of challenging us with separate renderings of human qualities, the characters are now gradually revealed to us. Amoral Miss Matthews begging Booth to tell her all he can of scenes of tenderness, Bondum the unscrupulous bailiff arguing that he knows what is owing to a gentleman, Colonel James telling his wife not to cross him in his love affairs, his wife telling him that Amelia is both too short and too tall, Dr Harrison enjoying Amelia's flattery and Colonel Bath praising Shakespeare as a very pretty poet indeed, are all examples of characters expressing themselves in such individual ways that what remains in one's memory is not a dream image or a caricature but at least a sketchy impression of a lifelike person.

Trent's argument with Booth over whether it is worth lending your wife to a nobleman if it can help your career is worth quoting from. 'I think, when I am talking to you, I talk to a man of sense and to an inhabitant of this country, not to one who dwells in a land of saints,' he says, and a little later, 'You know best what friends you have to depend upon; but, if you have no other pretensions than you merit, I can assure you you would fail, if it was possible you could have ten times more merit than you have' (*Amelia,* II, pp. 223-4). This has a perfectly and painfully true ring as a pronouncement by a character emancipated from the moral categories of the author, who would normally have worked a judgment into it, if only by means of a few unmistakable over-statements. Trent is life itself, and a tender-minded reader might well feel cornered and frightened by him, wondering if the author no longer had any relief to offer.

The relief is there, even in *Amelia,* provided by the hero and heroine and by some aspects of Dr Harrison — by the parts of the novel that present life as the author thinks it should be, for us to cling to. They feel the right feelings and say the right words. They may not be lifelike, and their conversations with each other may be moral tracts, but that need not stop them being a comfort to the reader.

At the same time they are not without their share in the living side of the novel. When Amelia is annoyed with Mrs Atkinson for impersonating her at the masquerade and furthering the career of her own husband, Mrs Atkinson fails to see what was wrong with that. It is an innovation that occurs several times in this novel: two characters interpreting actions and events differently, and neither of them being obviously and entirely wrong.' "I do not know, Mrs Booth," answered the other, "whence this great superiority over me is derived; but, if your virtue gives it you, I would have you to know, madam, that I despise a prude as much as you can do —" ' (*Amelia,* II, p. 231).

None of these innovations are entirely new. Disputes between characters who neither of them quite win occur in the earlier novels, and so do stretches of dialogue between characters who sound like just themselves, without exaggeration. What is characteristic of the earlier dialogues is not principally that they fail to observe a plausible resemblance to the sort of person they represent. It is that Fielding's enjoyment of the literary artefact shifts the weight of his representation away from the immediate contact with living reality to the independent verbal image, which draws its sustenance from reality but was not expected to conform to its daily proportions. This is not to say that all his talk about writing history and showing people in their true colours can be written off as an attempt to mislead the reader. He did bring in unfamiliar elements of reality from the first, but in Amelia he went further than he had done before, leaving out his dialogue games and his picture descriptions and making his story almost entirely out of what his characters needed to say to each other.

This development is not necessarily progress and development. Fielding's contemporaries did not see it as such, nor did many later readers. The only incontrovertible thing one can say about it is that it was the direction in which he moved, in his attempt to give the novel more meaning than it had had in *Pamela,* and to adapt it to his changed view of life; and the next thing is that it coincided with the direction in which the novel had to go, or at least did go.[11]

An interest in Fielding would be precariously based on an impression that he went from strength to strength. It would be better to say that jettisoning certain qualities gave him a better chance as well as a need to develop others.

It would also be difficult to maintain that whatever he did he could not help adding new riches to our cultural heritage. However conscientiously one tries to put everything in his novels in its true perspective, long stretches of them make lively and hospitable entertainment without persuading us that we become more acutely aware of the complexities and subtleties of human experience. Apart from some pleasant details of character and a number of explosive incidents it is not easy to see what the events of Fielding's novels, as distinct from his discursive writing on human nature and literature, contribute to our vision of life on earth. So much of his descriptions and his dialogue slips lightly from our memory that one remains doubtful after several re-readings whether one is looking for the wrong thing, or in the wrong way. Is there more complexity than our jaded palates can distinguish after another two centuries of novels? Or should we appreciate the work more strictly in terms of form and structure?

iv

Fielding never attempted to make us believe in his characters. So much is clear, and it has been noted by many critics, not always in a spirit of approval. 'If you had told Flaubert or Conrad in the midst of their passionate composings that you were not convinced of the reality of Homais or Tuan Jim, as like as not they would have called you out and shot you, and in similar circumstances Richardson would have shown himself extremely disagreeable. But Fielding, Thackeray, and Meredith would have cared relatively

11. In Ian Watt's words: '... a new type of formal structure has been evolved in which the plot attempts only to embody the ordinary processes of life and in so doing becomes wholly dependent on the characters and the development of their relationships' (*The Rise of the Novel,* p. 319), this direction is satisfactorily defined; although on the other hand, while praising Fielding for enlarging the scope of the novel, Watt did not allow him any credit for helping to evolve this new structure.

little about that,' wrote Ford Madox Ford, aligning himself with the execution squad.[12] His attitude on this point was similar to that of Henry James who blamed Trollope for admitting that his characters were make-believe. 'He admits that the events he narrates have not really happened, and that he can give his narrative any turn his reader may like best. Such a betrayal of a sacred office seems to me, I confess, a terrible crime,' wrote James.[13] He does not seem to have blamed Fielding for a comparable practice, perhaps because it did not offend him as much if an author pretended to argue that history forced him to record the truth, whatever some readers might have liked to hear.

The preference for an illusion of reality in the novel may look slightly old-fashioned. · Many readers still enjoy following the adventures of allegedly real people, but thinking of those hundreds of thousands of novels that have been published all with genuine illusions in them one does begin to feel oppressed by their weight, and to sympathize with authors who admit that their story is just one they happen to have thought up. Those who do not admit it simply seem less honest, although in a different mood one could equally well find it pedantic to restate such an obvious truth all the time. In any case, for a novelist who wants to influence us or argue with us it seems the most reasonable practice to take his characters through as many controversial situations as his narrative will permit, and to explain the point whenever necessary. However, there is a snag, clearly defined by Ian Watt: '... the organization of the narrative into an extended and formal structure will tend to turn the protagonists into passive agents;' to make up for that, he says, we may find 'a variety of minor characters, whose treatment will not be hampered in the same way by the roles which they are allotted by the complications of the narrative design.'[14]

This was written about Fielding, and it fits him perfectly. Much as one may think novel-reading a more adult pastime when it confronts us with the world outside as well as with its own fiction than when it carries us off into dream worlds, his leading

12. *The English Novel* (1930), p. 89, quoted in Claude Rawson (ed.), Henry Fielding, *A Critical Anthology*, p. 346.
13. Henry James, 'The Art of Fiction,' *Selected Literary Criticism*, p. 80.
14. Watt, *The Rise of the Novel*, p. 318.

characters all suffer from mechanization. Perhaps a writer who wants to air his views on the world outside had better put them in an essay after all? But Fielding did write essays both in his novels and elsewhere, and clearly felt that they did not contain all he had to say. The point about stories is that they enable the writer to bring up events of different sizes and weights that would cohabit uneasily in a discursive piece of prose; even if the characters have to be made to toe the line to prevent them confusing the issue, they enlarge the field of discussion.

With Fielding, the characters are kept in check by an artificial story which matches the pictures of his pictorial writing and the phrases of his dialogue. The structure was coherent enough for reliable traditional romances, but he combined it with newer forms of dialogue and to some extent of description. At moments the dialogue sounds like a written sermon, and only seconds later it might have been tape-recorded from a private conversation; a little later again the participants rattle on like stage comedians. The difficulty for the modern reader is that he does not always know how to recognize different styles and may make faults of interpretation; but there is no doubt about the difference, in the styles as well as in the response sought from the reader.

The least variable element, unfortunately but explicably, were the good people at the top. Fielding could not do without them, even when in *Amelia* some of his plotting had become more relaxed. As an extension to Watt's view one could suggest that the restriction of the leading characters to roles of passive agents, although originally encouraged by the structure, had another motivation which enabled it to continue on its own. Whether the structure was tight or loose, Fielding needed the final triumph of the good to give meaning to his narrative; and having to be so particularly and always visibly good they could not be left to chance. They had to submit.

It is true that in *Tom Jones* and more markedly in *Amelia* some of the women's goodness is superior to that of the men, resting on a secure foundation of homage-to-Charlotte. Fielding's next hero after Booth might well have been a plausibly dubious figure, if the line from Joseph Andrews onwards had been continued. Tom is not as faultless as Joseph, but he inspired Irvin Ehrenpreis to write: 'If the essential line of action in *Tom Jones* does support a special doctrine, ... it is that successful courtship of a good woman is at once an education in virtue and the highest test of character.'[15] Poor Booth's personality does little to confirm this strange notion, and Fielding might well have arrived at a more rational view of the matter as expressed in Robert Graves's lines: 'Why have such scores of lovely, gifted girls/Married impossible men?'[16] As it was, the passive agents of good remained intact when the plot structure had begun to crumble. A casual reader might suggest that it had begun to crumble before, because *Joseph Andrews* does not look nearly as tightly organized as either *Jonathan Wild* or *Tom Jones*. This is only partially true. Douglas Brooks has argued persuasively for the presence in the book of a central accent, even if it is a shifting one; he has also indicated some numerical patterns that would be certain to escape the reader who did not have his eye specially trained on such matters.[17]

Ideally, the patterns should help to strengthen the substance of the main themes of the book and rub in its sense more firmly. They may work like that for some readers, but often they look more like means to help the author to get his story properly set up. Brooks reasons that in Chapter 12 of Book I of *Joseph Andrews,*

> Joseph is robbed and rescued; in II.12 he and Fanny are reunited; in III.12 Fanny is rescued from rape and reunited with Joseph. The pattern is, in fact, a cumulative one: III.12 combines the motifs (robbery, reunion) that occur separately in I.12 and II.12. And so insistent is it that it almost forces us to predict what Fielding has in store for IV.12.[18]

It seems unlikely that any modern reader would show such insight. Perhaps Fielding's contemporaries were more acute, but if they thought the pattern strengthened the novel they would simply be wrong; all it did was to make the characters more mechanical. With a superb twist, says Brooks, Joseph and Fanny are reunited again but in an unwelcome way by being thought brother and sister. As an element in an abstract design this twist might be superb; for a novel-reader who was hoping to find a resemblance

15. Ehrenpreis, *Tom Jones,* p. 55.

16. Robert Graves, 'A Slice of Wedding-cake,'*Poems Selected by Himself,* Harmondsworth 1961.

17. Douglas Brooks, *Number and Pattern in the Eighteenth-century Novel,* pp. 65-91.

18. ibid., p. 72.

to living experience it would make more sense if the evidence of the family relationship had been confirmed in the remaining pages, and forced the lovers unhappily apart. Instead, new evidence of events after Joseph's birth puts it right, leaving the couple looking more passive and mechanical than ever. There was never much hope for these two, both of them too perfect to exist; but there are moments when one might have thought they would begin to move and speak. In the end, the structure wins.

In *Tom Jones* the hero is not quite as spotless as his predecessor; but the rest of the structure is all the more inescapable. One is frequently conscious of the work that must have gone into getting all these events to happen at the right times in the right places. Countless subtleties of possible patterning come to light in Brooks's researches; some of them might have surprised Fielding, but it would not do to establish the dividing-line between true and fanciful guided only by some vaguely modern good sense. In any case, the structure of three times six books is surely beyond dispute, as is the placing of the story of the Man of the Hill right in the middle; and the intricate design of the plot, with or without numerical balance, has been one of the wonders of English literature from the moment of its publication.

Fielding's constructive ingenuity is likely to be enjoyed most by readers of detective fiction — not primarily because of the elements of mystery and detection, although these will also help, but because of the attention to floods of tiresome detail.

> But, having had a more particular account from Honour of this man afterwards at Gloucester, and hearing of the great expedition he usually made in travelling, for which (as hath been before observed) he was particularly famous; recollecting likewise, that she had overheard Mrs Honour inform him that they were going to Gloucester, she began to fear lest her father might, by this fellow's means, be able to trace her to that city; wherefore if she should there strike into the London road, she apprehended he would certainly be able to overtake her. She therefore altered her resolution; ... she resolutely left Mrs Whitefield's about eleven at night, and striking directly into the Worcester road, within less than four hours arrived at that very inn where we last saw her (*Tom Jones*, II, p. 240).

Such complexities can only please those who enjoy them for

their own sake. They do not convey a sense of either outward adventure or inner experience; and there are too many of them.

> When Mr Allworthy and his nephew went to meet Mr Western, Mrs Miller set forwards to her son-in-law's lodgings, in order to acquaint him with the accident which had befallen his friend Jones; but he had known it long before from Partridge (for Jones, when he had left Mrs Miller, had been furnished with a room in the same house with Mr Nightingale) (*Tom Jones*, III, p. 267).

It is not only compared to later novelists with a smoother talent for sorting out their plots that such labyrinthine explanations look incompetent and make the reader want to think of something else. Fielding himself demonstrates, in his happier moments, an ability to use twists in his narrative as means to reveal traits of character and conduct. When Sophia tells Harriet Fitzpatrick the story of her recent life up to their meeting at the very fair promising inn which was probably at Meriden, she mentions everyone except Tom.

> This I will neither endeavor to account for nor to excuse. Indeed, if this may be called a kind of dishonesty, it seems the more inexcusable, from the apparent openness and explicit sincerity of the other lady. But so it was (*Tom Jones*, II, p. 283).

With its invitation to do our own interpreting of Sophia's reserve, this passage makes us feel so imaginative that it will not occur to us to complain of complication. Admittedly it deals only with a simple quirk of her own, and not with the comings and goings of a whole group of characters; and inevitably there are more often several characters competing for our attention in *Tom Jones*. In Joseph Andrews and again in Amelia, the story is centred on two characters all the way along. Tom on the other hand, although he can claim to be the most important figure in the book, has a variety of rivals to contend with: Sophia and Mrs Honour, and Western and his sister and Blifil, in the front row; and even in the second row several sets of characters operate more independently than anybody in the other books except, for a few moments, Lady Booby and Mrs Slipslop; these include Thwackum and Square, Lady Bellaston and Lord Fellamar, Mrs Miller and her daughters and the Nightingale family. There is little doubt that Fielding enjoyed juggling with groups of people, and he tried to communicate the spirit in which he exercised this art to his reader; but the times when one goes along with him find themselves nicely balanced with those when one wishes the story would be straightened out for a change.

The contrast with *Amelia* is marked, not only because there the narrative centre is firmly situated in the Booths, and a need to tie up loose ends occurs only on rare occasions like the beginning of Book XII. With no more of the excitement of journeys and arrivals to take our minds off human failings, no engagements and marriages in prospect, and only a sluggish social round for people's deceptions to be practised in instead of the whirl of hope and greed of *Tom Jones*, it is disturbing to see what a dark and confined world Fielding evokes. The boisterous story-teller has had a breakdown, and shows us life in the dry shades of grey that he probably always saw, as testified by many of his characters in the earlier books, but that we thought need not be taken seriously as he was so obviously enjoying himself at the same time.

Shreds and fragments of an old-style narrative structure can still be observed, in addition to the standard happy couple destined for fulfilment. They do not join up to determine the shape of the story. The narrative sags, as people talk all the time and have no need to act with urgency; and the background visible behind them is mostly Newgate prison, a sponging-house and a probably denuded room in the Booth's apartment. Instead of crooks to condemn, we have disillusioned people with soured marriages and get-rich-quick schemes. Poor Booth, burdened with a credulous nature and a gambling urge, appears locked up in a life without future; when he is finally saved, it is too late and too improbable for comfort.

In the sort of novel which is 'perhaps most typical' of the genre in general, said Ian Watt, the Aristotelian priority of plot over character has been reversed: 'It is Defoe and above all Richardson who provide this tradition with its archetypes, just as it is Fielding who provides that for the opposite tradition.'[19] One could say that this is less true in *Amelia* than it was before, and that the subsidiary characters are on the march. Although they did not get far enough to reverse the priority, there are grounds for disputing that Fielding

---

19. Watt, *The Rise of the Novel*, p. 319; cf. above, p. 80 n. 11.

deserves to be regarded as the patron saint of 'the opposite tradition.' He might equally well be seen as its destroyer: trying to make it work, finding it inadequate, and breaking out.

v

Not to admire the construction of Fielding's novels is the cruellest thing one can do to them. The artificiality of some of the pictorial description, and the awkward poses it demands of the characters, could be justified by arguing that this is how he wanted it, and that moreover it is possible to enjoy these poses and appreciate them in their own right. The stiffness of parts of the dialogue lends itself less easily to positive appreciation, but no writer can be at the top of his form all the time and there are more important things in life than invariable felicity of expression.

The most important thing in a novel is precisely the overall effect that will sweep faults of detail along without losing its power and meaning. When we finish we should feel that our awareness of the sum of human experience is at least slightly different from when we had just begun. Quibbles over matters of description and dialogue can easily sound pedantic by the side of that major question, and will have to be wrapped up in fashionable terminology to seem significant.

If it is said, or very nearly said, that the structure of a particular novel hampers the life of the characters and forces them to behave artificially, it begins to look like a total condemnation. Something can be saved with the help of historical insight, by saying that like his type of pictorial description such structures were what the author wanted and that what looks like dead wood can be returned to life if we put in more study of his times. We can also reverse an earlier process and concentrate on the parts that will make up for the faults of the whole.

The fact remains that Fielding's novels go back and forth between a stiffness that belongs to the romances of the late seventeenth century and a suppleness of psychology and technique that no later novelist has improved on; and that even apart from taste it would be plausible to regard examples of the latter quality, which show his vision and not just his technique, as the most valuable part of the work. Now and then a temptation makes itself felt to think of the novel form as gradually imposing itself with historical inevitability on those who practised the writing of long stories. This notion can only be defensible when applied to one particular practitioner if he is obviously engaged in devising subtler ways of differentiating between his characters and their motivations; it cannot be presented as a phenomenon in the whole of English or any other literature. With Fielding one should also take into account a growing desire to emulate Richardson in handling intimate experience, a growing doubt about human nature eroding the division between good and bad, and at the end of his career a lack of time, preventing the erection of an elaborate structure in advance.

In any case novels depend on conventions for their survival. The conventions may differ somewhat at different times, and be more restrictive or less so, but it is not as if we could speak from a knowledge of what a proper novel is like once the genre has come into its own. We can only suggest that some ways of doing it seem to put less strain on the material supplied by experience than others. There are novels, Fielding's which are easy to summarize among them, where it will not be too difficult to propose ways of relieving the strain by altering the plot here and there. It would not have pleased the helpless novelists, but nobody is going to take it seriously enough for lasting damage to be inflicted on their works. Proposing alternative plots might do more harm to criticism than to the art of the novel, if it led to critics indulging themselves with casual projects which they would never be called upon to implement.

It might not be a commendable general practice, but used gently and discreetly it can help to clarify points. As *Joseph Andrews* could with luck and good writing become a more moving story if Joseph and Fanny were kept apart at the end, so one could also improve *Tom Jones*. It would be destructive to keep Tom and Sophia apart, not so much for themselves as for the reader who would miss the exquisite scene when Sophia, having offered a clear survey of her arguments against an early marriage, responds to her father's suggestion that she get married nonetheless with: 'I will obey you. There is my hand, Mr Jones' (III, p. 365). Blifil however, being a poor creation, could be redesigned without any loss. If he was a sociable little fellow with an average eye to the main chance, and if Allworthy's selection of him as his heir was based only on the family relationship, both characters would have a better start in their literary lives; and it would not be beyond human ingenuity to devise a means by which Tom, having run away because he felt too poor to deserve Sophia, could come into some money, either from Allworthy or from some other source.

In *Amelia* the obvious candidate for improvement would be the heroine, who could retain her sweet temperament much of the time but should vary it with outbursts of anger born from the insecurity of her life with Booth, and with consequent consideration of a need to leave him, for the sake of herself and the children; and she might well, dramatically if not irrevocably, decide to do that when she comes into her falsely withheld inheritance.

Both novels could have benefited from these changes, if Fielding had been availabe to re-write them, because they would both lose some of their stiffness and artificiality. As it is they will continue to suffer from those defects, to such an extent that it is impossible to take their stories seriously. Fielding, nevertheless, is still with us. Trying to account for this immortality by defining the qualities of his best-known work does not yield entirely satisfactory results. In the end one comes to suspect that what counts most may be not the work, but the personality behind it.

IV FIELDING HIMSELF

i

Saying that in Fielding's novels the author's presence always remains recognizable is not in itself enough to distinguish him from other novelists. Hard though some of them may have striven to depersonalize and universalize the work of art, and to neutralize the narrator's voice, only those who were so commonplace as to lack a style of their own have ever been dissolved in their fictions. Wide differences occur, however, even if they are only of degree. Characters and the relations between them can acquire such density that their creator becomes difficult to discern. This does not mean that he has become intangible. Parts at least of his own nature and vision are likely to have found their way into his characters, and to be half-hidden in his implied judgments. To understand his work thoroughly, it is worth seeing how much of him we can plausibly define in it.

It may be worth admitting that this is not the only way to improve one's understanding of fiction. The essence and value of a novel can be sought elsewhere than in its role as spokesman for the imagination of the writer. Even in the case of Fielding it is possible to try a more objective interpretation; but the results are likely to be unsatisfactory, in dealing with an author who intrudes so persistently.

Technically it would not be out of the question for someone as intrusive as he is to create substantial characters that cut him off from our view, and a complexity of relationships that absorbed all our interest; but he has not done so. The characterization even of Adams and Tom Jones is thin, which is to say that one immediately recognizes their author behind them. Whether funny or brave or vain or firm, Adams never suggests enough inner life to make us look twice. Tom has only his infidelities to make us wonder, and although these are not to be despised they are insufficient to give him his full weight as a character. Very few readers can ever have been reminded of Tom Jones by any person living or dead. There is not enough of him; he consists of an outline of a figure, without a distinct face.

The relations between the characters are correspondingly thin. It is hard to think of a less colourful love affair than that between Joseph and Fanny. If one seeks compensating colour in the friendship of Adams and Joseph, all that can be said about them in the end is that they are travelling-companions from the same village who are prepared to defend each other under attack.

Much the same is true of life in the Allworthy household, where the long ascendancy of young Blifil in spite of his repellent looks is simply an unlikely story, half helped out by the casual comment that of course Allworthy could not see things as clearly as we do. The exchanges between Squire Western and his sister are engagingly lifelike and make excellent dialogue, but they are always on the same lines and represent human conflict in a very small way.

The Booths' domestic life is equally narrowly documented, with evidence of fecklessness and sweetness but little to show us the effect of these qualities on each other. When it comes to complex relations *Amelia* nonetheless goes somewhat further than its predecessors, with its Jameses and Atkinsons. Although there is little detail, there is a suggestion that these people's lives do not lend themselves to summing-up in straightforward terms. Here at last are some characters that need looking at twice.

What this amounts to is a further way of saying that the lasting strength of Fielding's novels cannot be satisfactorily explained by the fictional vitality in them. The lovableness of Adams, the preposterousness of Mrs Slipslop, the roughness of Western and the femininity of Amelia are invoked in vain. Nor is it much use pointing to the firmness of moral purpose that is manifest in the treatment of the characters, or to the incredibly large number of wheels that have been fitted into the machinery of *Tom Jones*. Disappointing though it may be when we seek to define Fielding's importance, after long and thoughtful discussion the parts of his novels that still come first to mind are the slapstick scenes. When Fielding's characters cause havoc in kitchens and bedrooms, flinging pots of coloured liquid at each other and tussling with unidentified interlopers in the dark, critical distinctions become powerless. We may be too easily impressed, ignorant as most of us are of what really goes on in such spontaneous indoor riots. For better or worse, these scenes form an essential part of our image of Fielding.

Together with them we find a wide variety of other fragments and details that help to keep his fictions alive. At the same time we discover a considerable amount of description and judgment of human nature that will not stand up under scrutiny; and there are stretches of pointless narrative that can only hold our attention for historical reasons.

This would be very nearly the sum total of the value of Fielding's novels for us if we only had their stories to reckon with. It would be amazing that we can bring ourselves to spend so much time on them, if we were not aware of something else at work: the author's or the narrator's personality, both in its handling of the story and as an object of interest in itself. 'Fielding's art,' in the words of John Preston, 'is in the nature of a dialogue carried on across the boundaries between fiction and reality. His writing is addressed to the real world through an imagined one, to real feelings through a fictional narrative, to the real reader by an imagined narrator.'[1]

Something like such a dialogue with the outside world must be recognized before we can make sense of Fielding's work. Among various refinements that one might attempt is a modification of the idea of a 'dialogue,' always an unsatisfactory term to use when one of the parties does all the talking and the other cannot reply, only respond. It could also be disputed that Fielding's narrator is continuously an imagined one. There are times when he is indistinguishable from the author speaking for himself; perhaps at other times one may say that the imagined narrator contains more Fielding than the author pretending to address us directly could.

In any case, it is by discovering the true image of Fielding real and imagined that we may hope to find his significance rather than by attempts to overestimate the stories he is telling. For some of the time, in his introductions to the novels or to parts of them, the fictional element is ignored: he is addressing us in his own name, or conventionally disguised as *we*. In those parts we are at least as

1. John Preston, 'Is there a Good Book on Fielding?', *Essays in Criticism*, XXI no. 1 (1971), 91-100.

directly in touch with him as in the articles he wrote for his newspapers, from *The Champion* to the *Covent Garden Journal.* Often he can be said to produce more of a living voice in his personal appearances in the novels, where he is the author who wants a word in our ear, than in articles and essays where his discussion of general matters in general terms is apt to make him sound like an editorial committee even in the first person singular.[2]

In addition to the introductory pieces, some of which could serve as essays or articles in their own right, the author often appears in the narrative chapters themselves, commenting on the action or on his handling of it or promising further shocks and surprises. 'In all of his work, satiric and non-satiric, Fielding is reluctant to leave the reader or viewer to see the connotations for himself; he consistently informs him that this *is* a farce, and what its significance may be.'[3] And even this does not mark the limit of Fielding's presence in his fiction. In fact, having seen him intrude so frequently, one begins to hear him in every line; not just to know that he is behind it all, but to be conscious of it all the time. 'The point is that the moral and social commentator, Fielding the essayist, he is always present; ... the narrative is everywhere one weave, steadily editorializing, sometimes conspicuously, some-times unobtrusively.'[4]

There is no need to improve on Robert Alter's description of the novels as 'one weave,' rather than as a narrative interrupted by discursive passages. At first sight it may seem less true, or to make less sense in the case of *Amelia,* where there are no separate chapters for the author to address us and where the impression might be that he is inclined 'to leave the reader or viewer to see the connotations for himself.' After some adaptation, one recognizes him as easily as before. It may be true, as Arthur J. Hassall has

2. 'But in reality the knowledge of human nature is not learnt by living in the hurry of the world. True genius, with the help of a litle conversation, will be capable of making a vast progress in this learning; and indeed I have observed, there are none who know so little of men, as those, who are placed in the crouds, either of business or pleasure' (*Preface to Familiar Letters on David Simple,* 1747, quoted in Ioan Williams (ed.), *The Criticism of Henry Fielding,* p. 134).

3. Ronald Paulson, *Satire and the Novel in Eighteenth Century England,* p. 92.

4. Robert Alter, *Fielding and the Nature of the Novel,* p. 34.

said,[5] that in *Amelia* the dramatic narrative form and the authorial commentary get in each other's way instead of supporting each other, and one may also have to agree with Robert Alter when he says that 'Fielding's sense of audience, so essential to the achievement of *Joseph Andrews* and *Tom Jones,* is simply uneven in this novel.'[6]

For the present purpose, the main point is that we recognize him nonetheless.

> In fact, if we regard this world only, it is the interest of every man to be either perfectly good or completely bad. He had better destroy his conscience than gently wound it (*Amelia,* I, p. 176).

> But, though he was a gay man, he was in reality so fond of his Amelia that he thought of no other woman; wherefore though not absolutely a Joseph, as we have already seen, yet could he not be guilty of premeditated inconsistency (*Amelia,* II, p. 193).

The sound of such sentences is as familiar as the experience of being steered towards what the author considers the proper judgment of the situation. Unbalanced or uneven though his narration may have become, he is unmistakably the same man. If one wanted to persuade a hesistant reader to take up *Amelia,* one would not plead the loveliness of the heroine, nor the loosely assembled foibles or her husband. One would not insist on the need to appreciate the desperately black world that came to replace the roughness of the earlier books; nor would it be tactful to make too much, for a new reader, of the ambiguity of characterization.

The argument would be, do not miss this sound of Fielding who still, in his last novel, invites if not a dialogue, a response.

ii

Looking for Fielding's personality in his novels the first version of it which we encounter is inevitably mixed up with his narrating *persona.* 'Of course, the narrator in these chapters is not in a strict sense the "real" Fielding; it is a specially contrived mouthpiece for

5. Anthony J. Hassall, 'Fielding's Amelia: Dramatic and Authorial Narration,' *Novel,* V no. 3 (1971), 225-233.

6. Alter, *Fielding and the Nature of the Novel,* p. 161.

the author, emphasizing some of his own qualities and suppressing others. We know that Fielding's own moods and personal circumstances were sometimes at variance with the tone of his disquisitions in the novel. Like Mozart he was capable of producing sublime comedy whilst his own life took a grim or tragic course.'[7] Pat Rogers, in these words, sums up the consensus about Fielding's narrator. However, if the narrator is not the whole of Fielding, he cannot help being part of him. We would miss much evidence if we chose to go for his hidden deeper personality only. The showman who presents the novels to us may occasionally be carried away by his own words to a point where it becomes nearly impossible to recognize the responsible literary figure we came to see. There he is nonetheless, inimitable if not always in the sense of magnificent, because no one could be quite like him even in his style of being carried away.

Part of Fielding is that entertainer who appears before us in a multiplicity of guises in the novels. His most artificial role, in the sense that one cannot imagine him talking or writing like that without a funny face, is that of the mock-heroical classical imitator: 'thee, I call; of whom in a treckschuyte in some Dutch canal the fat ufrow gelt, impregnated by a jolly merchant of Amsterdam, was delivered' (*Tom Jones*, III, p. 32). At the other end of the scale, lines like 'Be it known, then, that the human species are divided into two sorts of people, to wit, "high" people and "low" people' (*Joseph Andrews*, p. 180), however ironical, can be pronounced perfectly casually, with the words doing their own work. Between these two, many shades of style occur, and the anxious modern critic may well find himself misjudging several of them, as he has no clear idea of how exuberantly or oddly Fielding could behave without overdoing it and embarrassing his listeners.

In any case, all the different styles are used by him and tell us things about him. It is true that they are of no great help if we try to imagine his private life. As Irving Ehrenpreis has put it, they are almost wholly internalized, revealing 'a moral and intellectual constitution but nothing more tangible.'[8] On the other hand, they do to some extent suggest to us how he looked and sounded when he was engaged in winning an audience; and the indefatigable

7. Pat Rogers, *Henry Fielding*, p. 163.
8. Irvin Ehrenpreis, *Henry Fielding*, p. 9.

quality of his efforts to win them is in itself typical of him. He was capable of addressing his readers as if they were literally sitting there, all listening to him at the same time. This may not be directly effective. In our silent rooms with the book before us, it tends to sound as if the author is speaking to all the others, while we look on. We are detached rather than involved, but that need not stop us enjoying the spectacle of that tireless man telling everybody where they should look and what they should realize.

While Fielding often appears like a showman first of all in his narrating role, it should be recognized that he is at the same time, and sometimes dominantly, a professional commentator on literary and moral affairs. An author ought to consider himself 'as one who keeps a public ordinary, at which all persons are welcome for their money,' and those who do not like what he offers deserve 'a right to censure, to abuse and to d — n their dinner,' he says in the first paragraph of *Tom Jones*. The reader begins to look forward to a feast of pure escapism, but he is soon undeceived, by references in the same chapter to the alderman of Bristol, to Mr Pope and to the Emperor Heliogabalus, and by such ambiguities as the announcement that after an initial presentation of human nature in a plain and simple manner the author will 'hereafter rash and ragoo it with all the high French and Italian seasoning of affectation and vice which courts and cities can afford.'

Evidently this author is not fired by just a humble desire to please; in the very first page he strikes the note of a man full of double meanings and controversy, and this is what he goes on to confirm in his dual role of entertainer and commentator. The introductory chapter to Book V, with Fielding at the top of his form, gives as brilliant an example of the mixture of the two roles as any. This is where the narrator explains that although there is no reason why he should, as it really means conceding a point to shallow jumped-up critics, he is prepared to justify these introductions by the rule of contrast: the serious setting off the comic, in the same way that on the stage the dull has often been effectively set off by a superlative degree of dulness, and that Homer was allowed sleepy passages by Horace's *Ars Poetica*, although it should not be assumed that authors actually write while sleeping: 'In this light, or rather in this darkness, I would have the reader to consider these initial essays' (*Tom Jones*, I, pp. 205-210).

It is this same chapter that opens with the immortal phrase

about the likelihood that the parts of the book that have given the author the greatest trouble may give the reader the least pleasure.[9] There is bound to be a touch of bitterness in that sort of self-mockery, but it is forgotten when the critics replace the unprofessional readers as the real models of literary incomprehension. From then on, Fielding is at the same time earnestly practising his art of anti-criticism, and enjoying himself by tickling the reader with the twists and turns he invents for his subject. Martin Battestin has pointed out that the notion of contrast as an aesthetic principle was far from being a new idea, as Fielding pretended.[10] But then neither does it really work as a justification for the introductory chapters. The contrast does not enhance our enjoyment of the narrative part of the novel. If anything the discursive chapters tend to put off lazy readers, as Fielding himself was the first to realize and says again at the end of the chapter: if the reader can find enough seriousness in other parts of the book 'he may pass over these, in which we profess to be laboriously dull.'

This profession is not to be trusted. The chapter is irresistibly entertaining, and must have given the author pleasure and satisfaction, too. Once again, he surprises us by saying the thing that is not, and puzzling the Houyhnhnms among us who fail to see the point of this preemptive strike against readers impatient at interruptions of their imaginative pleasure.

As for the serious content of this particular chapter, all through *Tom Jones* it looks as if Fielding felt easy and animated in his conflicts with the pedants who objected to his new style of writing. When he wrote *Joseph Andrews* it was less clear who the enemies were likely to be and what arguments they would produce; once they had declared themselves it was obvious that they did not have much of a case, only the strength of their numbers, and he handled them with self-assurance.

It seems possible to say that the opening of Book V shows Fielding in a dual role that suited his public ambition nicely: of entertainer and scourge of the critics. This was the author he liked us to see; but critics were far from being his only subject as a commentator. The one most directly related to the matter of organization of his new type of vision is that of the view of human

9. See above, p. 57.
10. In his Wesleyan Edition of *Tom Jones*, p. 212, no. 1.

nature in general, as distinct from that of a few privileged heroes and heroines. Fielding's ambition in this regard was not to reveal new motives and interpretations, but to liberate the image of human nature from misconceptions due largely to literary convention but also to inadequate philosophies. This accorded with his insistence that he was writing true stories instead of romances, showing humanity as it was, without any sacrifice of truth to narrative expediency. In actual fact he was capable of being unscrupulous about 'historical' plausibility when his stories required it, particularly when they approached their conclusion; but except in cases where it was too inconvenient, his claim can be allowed to stand. If readers should be shocked at the information that Sophia was less upset about Tom's having spent the night with another woman than by reports that he had talked irresponsibly about herself, he reminded 'such persons' that he was writing a history, and 'I am not obliged to reconcile every matter to the received notions concerning truth and nature' (*Tom Jones,* II, p. 332). It would be ungrateful to complain about a historical approach that can produce results like these, even in the case of Amelia who after Atkinson's confession that he has loved her for years and hopes he may kiss her hand, 'left the house with a confusion on her mind that she had never felt before' (*Amelia,* II, p. 276).

As a supplementary feature of Fielding's claim to historical veracity, there is his knack of announcing to the reader that certain conversations took place but will not be reported as they would bore him. When he does this too often,[11] it becomes a little embarrassing, but in itself it is a plausible idea. A true report of human affairs will inevitably contain many dull bits, and we should be grateful to the historian for sparing us these, particularly when he wants to act as entertainer at the same time. Nothing could be more natural for a narrator who is out to amuse us than to say that 'as nothing passed which in the least concerns us or our reader, we shall not suffer ourselves to be diverted by it' (*Tom Jones,* III p. 47). In this respect again, he combines his two roles to excellent effect.

11. For instance in *Tom Jones,* where in Bk.XIII, ch.iv, by which time we are fully conversant with this practice, he does it three times in rapid succession.

When the commentator in Fielding goes beyond the subjects of literary construction and characterization and deals with human affairs in a wider sense, the entertainer loses some of his exuberance. This does not mean that he can no longer be seen in the same role. It has long been an accepted technique in the presentation of shows to make the laughter alternate with serious or tearful interludes; in this respect the effect of contrast is often more satisfactory than in the mixing of stories with essays.

Most of the occasions when this effect can be studied in Fielding are when his commentator deals with matters of morality, in social organization or in private relations. The purest indictment of social immorality occurs in *Jonathan Wild.* The hero himself is so evil that attempts to reform him could only end in absurdity, but the Londoners round him who allow him to regard his misdeeds as signs of greatness might do better if they saw things more clearly. His victims, Heartfree and his wife, are too naive and soft to defend themselves, let alone to provide a moral alternative.

The alternative comes in *Joseph Andrews,* where the wickedness is generalized in the background instead of individualized in front, and Joseph and Fanny and Adams suggest that goodness may also occur in sturdy natures. *Tom Jones* repeats the pattern of a promising young couple and an older gentleman, against a background less black but as unlikely to show moral improvement as the Andrews world. In *Amelia* the pattern occurs again, but with even less hope and promise because the good people have lost their bounce.

In none of the novels does the spectrum of humanity displayed in the characters justify optimism in the reader; but the author, or narrator, is always there to point out what is wrong with the world, and to make us feel while we read that we will naturally do better than that. In the social context, what would be required of us is strangely little by the standards of the present age when many people regard the organization of society on the basis of a radical theory as a self-evident necessity. As a man of his time, Fielding could hardly be expected to have gone in for radicalism, but in some moods he was something of an egalitarian. Not only did he display, at such moments, a classical contempt for wordly distinctions and benefits, which enabled him to present Mr Wilson's placid existence as an ideal. He also enjoyed cutting the upper classes and the rich down to size in his work, and he showed the vigour of his egalitarian streak when in 1747 he married Mary Daniel who had been his first wife's maid — 'his natural spirits gave him rapture with his cook-maid,' as Lady Mary Wortley Montagu wrote.[12] This disposition did not make him a forerunner of the radical thinkers of the later eighteenth century. What he would be thinking of would be most like a general relaxation that could result from individuals in privileged positions becoming more honest and generous and appreciative of merit and honesty; more like Mr Allworthy and Dr Harrison, and less like Lady Booby and *Amelia's* Noble Lord. It would be a help if people became more perceptive about human nature, he argued in his *Essay on Knowledge of Characters of Men*[13] which is mostly concerned with the damage done by hypocrisy and pretence.

Fielding's ideas for a better society did not go beyond moral exhortation of its individual members, along lines which were not his alone. 'Underlying many of the most memorable characters in eighteenth-century literature — Sir Roger de Coverley, Squire Allworthy, Dr Harrison, Sir Charles Grandison, Dr Primrose, Uncle Toby, and, of course, Parson Adams — the theory of the good man reduces his essential characteristics to two: personal chastity (representative of the temperate discipline of the passions) and social charity.'[14] Fielding's own added ingredient was Good Nature as represented by Tom Jones. This simple-sounding notion has got him into trouble over the centuries with critics who assumed that all he wanted was for people to be nice and friendly. He was not really as simple as that, realizing that some firm support would be needed and finding it in religion and in reason. Good nature provided an adequate standard by which to condemn all sorts of unpleasant people, as Fielding did throughout his career, scornfully or casually or exuberantly or dejectedly. The image of the Good Man may never have been strong enough to inspire a faith and cause conversions; but even if his only adherents were the previously converted, it could be seen as a valuable function for a novelist to put new heart into them, rather than leaving the ground free for the Blifils and the Noble Lords.

In any case, Fielding kept recommending his good man all

12. Wilbur R.Cross, *The history of Henry Fielding*, II, pp. 60-1.
13. H.K. Miller (ed.), *Miscellanies, Vol. I*, pp. 153-178.
14. Martin C. Battestin, *The Moral Basis of Fielding's Art*, pp. 29-30.

through his writing career. It is one of his distinguishing marks: he is always at us with comments on the moral quality of his characters' behaviour. If he spreads these more thinly in *Amelia,* so that we are sometimes left to judge actions for ourselves or even to be in two minds about them, it does not mean that he has given up advising us. 'We desire, therefore, the good-natured and candid reader will be pleased to weigh attentively the several unlucky circumstances which concurred so critically that Fortune seemed to have used her utmost endeavors to ensnare poor Booth's constancy' (*Amelia,* I. p. 175). 'The doctor felt this sight as he ought' (*Amelia,* II, p. 125). 'Here I shall stop for one moment, and so, perhaps, will my good-natured reader; for surely it must be a hard heart which is not affected' (*Amelia,* II, p. 268).

Moreover, to stop us abusing the liberty he has occasionally allowed us in the course of the book Fielding metes out the most terrible punishments to his bad natures when he describes their further lives in the last chapter. Colonel James left his wife and went to live with Miss Matthews, who grew disagreeable and immensely fat; the Noble Peer and Mrs Ellison died from their favourite vices, sex for the one and drink for the other; Murphy was hanged, Miss Harris spent three years living on £ 50 p.a. and then died in a miserable manner; but Amelia, after several more years, was as handsome as ever. In his final novel Fielding's moral authority is undiminished. The rewards in the story itself: a preposterous piece of legal luck, and improverishment of Amelia's guilty sister, are negligible by the side of the narrator's additional verdicts. The moralist, not the novelist had the last word. He could not bring himself to let life take its course at the end of the story; he had to put his characters in their place according to merit.

This moral legalism is as inseparable from Fielding as his effort to liberate prose fiction and make it intellectually acceptable. If we had to read his novels entirely in moral terms, because we took him so seriously or because he had little else to offer, we might well find them impossible to get through, but fortunately much of the story and several of the characters have an existence outside his laws. The clearest view of Fielding's novels is achieved not by the analysis of his narrative but by listening to the voice of the narrator. No wonder he has usually been thought of as primarily a comic novelist, in spite of his elaborate pronouncements on the right way to live: they are only the author speaking for himself, and the story could survive without them.

Something similar is true of Fielding's concept of love. This is a subject on which he is speaking for himself in an even more personal sense than when he discusses good nature and prudence. The most notable example occurs in *Tom Jones,* where he reveals at an early stage that Sophia resembled most of all 'one whose image never can depart from my breast' and later on states even more firmly that 'under the fictitious name of Sophia' we are learning about 'the real worth which once existed in my Charlotte' (*Tom Jones,* I, pp. 146/7 & III, p. 30).

Although the heroines of *Jonathan Wild, Joseph Andrews* and *Amelia* are not so explicitly anchored in the author's private life, he suggests just as strongly that the love he talks about is his own. This involvement does not make it easier for him to let his imagination loose among the emotions and the actions of his lovers. Some novelists would feel shamelessly at ease in those circumstances. Fielding, frank though his style as an entertainer may be, never allows us an illusion that we are becoming intimate him. His exalted passages on the glories of love are not revelations of what goes on in himself or in his characters: they are formal celebrations, like wedding speeches. When Joseph sings his love for Fanny in his feverish delirium, or when they are married at last and he does not envy the noblest duke nor she the noblest duchess; when the beauties and other qualities of Sophia are eulogized in Book IV, chapter 2, and when Tom spends three hours reading and kissing her letter; when Booth waiting for Amelia in a garret would not have exchanged his 'poor lodgings for the finest palace in the universe' (*Amelia,* p. 75), and when Amelia throws her 'snowy arms around him' on his return home after borrowing £ 50 to pay off a gambling debt — all this is designed to appeal to the assembled company gathered round a happy couple rather than to the pensive reader in his armchair.

To vary the hyperbole of his passages on love Fielding occasionally used cutting references to the cold of heart, who would not know what he was talking about.

> We must now return to Mrs Heartfree, who passed a sleepless night in as great agonies and horror for the absence of her husband as a fine well-bred woman would feel at the return of hers from a long voyage or journey (*Jonathan Wild,* p. 83).

As their sensations, from their mutual silence, may be judged to
have been big for their own utterance, it cannot be supposed,
that I should be able to express them: and the misfortune is that
few of my readers have been enough in love ... (*Tom Jones,* III,
p. 81).

Several times, and particularly in *Tom Jones* when Blifil is held up
as the prime example of a loveless soul, negative versions of the
praises of love are used to bring the reader all the more inescapably
on the side of the lovers. They are put to tactical use, but that is
only a secondary role for them, the primary one being to express
Fielding's idea that the state of love is the highest that human
nature can attain to — or perhaps a better way of paraphrasing
this idea, and just as valid in Fielding's case, is that it is a state to
which only the best among us will ever attain.

Although it would be unjust to say that the love stories
themselves include no moving and revealing moments, it can be
argued that the narrator's pleas for love resound far more strongly
than anything the stories have to tell us. Not only is the subject
more talked about than shown in action: often in the description of
love scenes and even in the dialogue one hears the artist himself, in
one of his roles. ' "Fear, madam," says he, "easily runs into
madness; and there is no degree of fear like that which I feel of
offending you. How can I speak then? Nay, don't look angrily at
me: one frown will destroy me" ' (*Tom Jones,* I, p. 237). That is
Tom speaking. A few weeks later, when Lord Fellamar talks to her
in much the same vein ('For love hath so totally deprived me of
reason, that I am scarce accountable for any of my actions'),
Sophia 'answered this bombast (and very properly, I think) with a
look of inconceivable disdain' (*Tom Jones,* III, p. 155). The two
modes of address are impossible to tell apart, and neither of them
is typical of the character speaking. This is not how we should look
at the scenes, though. We are not concerned with these characters;
we are concerned with Fielding's vision of love.

One could go on finding examples of ways in which the author's
voice in these novels dominates the impression they create with
their incidents and characters; but these few major ones will
suffice. There is one further aspect that may be mentioned here,
although it is more doubtful than in the other cases that this shows
Fielding as he wanted us to see him. It is the urge to keep
interesting us all the time which one senses behind his continuous

personal presence in his novels. Tom Stoppard, the playwright, has observed something of the same nature in himself: 'But my preoccupation as writer, which possibly betokens a degree of insecurity, takes the form of contriving some sort of interest and colour into every line, rather than counting on the general situation having a general interest which will hold an audience.'[15] In *Tom Jones* particularly one recognizes a similar preoccupation. 'If we read straight through all the seemingly gratuitous appearances by the narrator, leaving out the story of Tom, we discover a running account of growing intimacy between the narrator and the reader, an account with a kind of plot of its own and a separate dénouement.'[16] The word intimacy comes a little awkwardly, after what was said about it here a moment ago; but Wayne Booth gives an impressively persuasive formulation to its dominant presence in the book.

Without dismissing his characters so frequently and occupying the stage on his own, the narrator is very nearly as inescapable in the other novels. Even in *Amelia* he addresses us directly often enough to keep us aware of his presence behind the scenes, and of the likelihood that he may pop out again any moment. Also he still cuts off a few dialogues with the explanation that the rest was not worthy of our interest, suggesting that what he is able to tell us will have more weight than the history of his characters on its own.

If one assumes that the insecurity which Stoppard suspected in himself may also have been present in Fielding, one would hesitate to class all the appearances of the dominant narrator's voice as firmly calculated and intentional. Perhaps it occurred to him sometimes that he got in the way of the story he was telling, as he did of course. Was he at all susceptible to a doubt whether the sort of reader he wanted to address could be expected to have all his attention absorbed by the sort of adventures met by Joseph and Tom; or was he wholly convinced that the story had plenty to offer anybody, but he could give it another dimension with his own reflections? It is an impossible choice for us to make with any certainty. Much would depend on how pleased Fielding was with himself, and there it is precisely the lack of intimacy that keeps us

15. Tom Stoppard, 'Ambushes for the Audience,' interview in *Theatre Quarterly* no. 14 (May-July 1974), 6.
16. Wayne C. Booth, *The Rhetoric of Fiction,* p. 216.

in doubt. Thinking how right Rebecca West was when she called him 'one of the most energetic beings who ever lived,'[17] one imagines that he did not waste much of his time being uncomfortable about himself.

This is not to say that he was entirely his own creation, summed up in the image he wanted us to see. In the dominant presence in the novels, one is bound also to observe elements not belonging to his plan, and the impression of his personality would be needlessly incomplete if we did not take these into account.

iii

The first thing to realize about Fielding's narrators is that they are not simply the author himself laying his heart on the table; the second is that the narrators in the different books, as Wayne Booth has pointed out, are not even identical with each other.[18] In the third place it should be observed that within each of the books the narrator varies his nature between the public entertainer set up for the occasion and somebody who sounds as if he might be the author in private. Listening to this latter voice, one finds evidence of attitudes and tastes that were not included in Fielding's self-display, because they were too intimate or too contradictory or for any other reason.

There would be little hope of getting general agreement on when the narrator sounds most like the real Fielding. The moments when he suggests most strongly the voice of the author himself are not necessarily those when he is most consciously involved with his ideas and emotions. They seem to occur rather in casual asides, such as that which describes Joseph Andrews as possessing 'an air which, to those who have not seen many noblemen, would give an idea of nobility' (*Joseph Andrews,* p. 48), or when he conversationally contradicts a current view of his times including, one might think, his own novels, in: 'I am convinced there never was less of love intrigue carried on among persons of condition, than now ... the true characteristic of the present beau monde is rather folly than vice' (*Tom Jones,* III, p. 95).

17. Rebecca West, review of the *London Journal* of Flora Tristan, *Sunday Telegraph,* 24 Jan. 1982.
18. Wayne C. Booth, *A Rhetoric of Irony,* p. 72.

It does not matter greatly at which points different readers imagine they see most of the narrator or of the creator. As long as the variations in the narrating tone are recognized we can all agree that the intended figure of Fielding-the-narrator is modified by traits that become apparent in spite of himself. It is not a case of a few touches of different colour here and there. The most obvious and the most far-reaching need for a modification of Fielding's narrating image occurs when one considers the background to his moral optimism and belief in good nature.

The optimism is far from consistent at the best of times. None of his other characters find the goodness of Heartfree or Joseph or Tom in the slightest degree infectious. They all remain exactly as they were, hidebound and hypocritical; and a vision that takes moral excellence to be irredeemably limited to about one character in twenty holds out little hope of a better future. Still, while the narrator remains cheerful the whole picture seems mostly full of good fun, and suggests a fair chance that the best will come out on top and the worst will, if not improve, be rendered more or less impotent.

The flame of this hope flickers only feebly in *Amelia*. Still, if one notes how cruel the destiny of the wicked turns out to be, an intention to give us some hope has to be assumed. At the same time we are bound to realize more strongly than before that the promise was never firm enough to survive outside the story it helped to cheer up. It is not only mean souls like Parson Trulliber, or the coachload of prudent citizens unwilling to assist the victim of a robbery who blacken our view of humanity. At least they are definably in the wrong, and one could imagine such people condemning their own conduct. The worse elements as far as any contribution to moral optimism is concerned are characters like Lady Booby who lets the village starve when she spends her time in London; the gentleman who talks about the infamy of cowards and runs home on hearing a woman shrieking from the bushes; and Pamela who, although Fanny was her equal in the past, considers this no longer true now that 'I am ... this gentleman's lady.' Such people would never detect anything wrong in their own attitudes; they are not primarily bad or weak, they are callous.

This callousness is less marked in *Tom Jones,* where much of the moral badness is absorbed by the serpentlike figure of Blifil. It is very dominant again in *Amelia;* Fielding's attitude to his characters may have changed since *Joseph Andrews,* but they themselves match the mentality of the uncharitable coachload. Whatever the distribution of the badness, and however variable the author's treatment, at no stage are we encouraged to hope for a better world, as a result of either stimulation by individual examples or challenge by social opportunity. When Fielding's sickly body on its way to Lisbon is jeered at by the sailors at Redriffe and he says that he has often contemplated human cruelty and inhumanity with concern, one knows what he means. He may not always have expressed it in those terms, but in retrospect the feeling was clearly present in all his work.

One of the starkest images to confirm Fielding's dismay at the human race occurs later on in that report of his last voyage when he describes Mrs Francis, the indignant landlady of Ryde. 'She was a short, squat woman; her head was closely joined to her shoulders,'' and so on,[19] creating a picture quite unlike reality in the eyes of Mrs Francis herself, who complained about it to a company of visitors the following year. She thought Fielding had been very unfair, considering the effort she had made for him, which included covering up the 'handsome looking-glass' in his room so that 'he might not be struck with his own figure.'[20] It seems possible that she may have been right at least to the extent that few other visitors would have found her quite so awful. Fielding had an unflattering eye for people who were not quick to please him, and in the last months of his life we may assume that pleasing him had become more difficult than in the days when he enjoyed himself in spite of everything. The quarrel with the ship's captain at a later stage of the voyage ('"Your cabin:" repeated he many times, "no, d-n me, 'tis my cabin. Your cabin! D-n me!"' — (*A Voyage to Lisbon,* p. 304) suggests a similar conclusion. The picture of the captain is less angry than that of Mrs Francis, but the tone of the quarrel belongs unmistakably in the eternal tradition of people getting in each other's way and persuading themselves it is the other who is aggressive and dishonest and unreasonable.

The later Fielding is not so much different from the early one as differently accented, making some of his partly hidden personality

19. See above, p. 48.
20. Cross, *The history of Henry Fielding,* III, p. 95.

more obvious. Reasoning back from 1754 one may wonder if his most excellent incarnations of good nature were not, rather than affirmations of a belief in our potential delightfulness, foils to set off more sharply our general inadequacy. Joseph Andrews could be interpreted as a human counterpart of the Houyhnhnms; but although this parallel may be valid theoretically, it does not help our understanding of his role in the novel. Joseph is humanity simplified, not abstraction humanized. In any case, we have no need to smooth over the contradictions in Fielding's vision. On the contrary: contradictions are essential, in him as in other people, and it is precisely when we become aware of the pattern of them that our image of him may begin to live.

If we restrict our idea of Fielding to the qualities that he himself was eager to advertise we end up with a suspiciously smooth image. For that same reason it is not just necessary but something of a relief to recognize that his egalitarian pose was not the whole story, only the part of it that he considered useful in correcting and teasing his readership. Few people can have been entirely taken in, and in general it is accepted that he was not a fundamental social reformer. As a child of his time, however, when egalitarianism was not in fashion, he looks distinctly liberal. The familiar passage in Book II, chapter 13 of *Joseph Andrews,* where he explains that the difference between high people and low people is in no sense one of character and ability, is a firm enough statement to make social climbers feel momentarily ridiculous. The cold single-mindedness of Lady Booby seems to point in the same direction; and so, from the other end, does the beauty and moral excellence of the low-born hero.

From the egalitarian point of view it is disappointing to learn that Joseph is of better birth than he seemed; and seven years later the excellent Tom turns out to be another such case. Perhaps these were solutions to narrative problems rather than expressions of genetic conviction, one might suggest. It would be wise to refrain from sweeping conclusions about them, but there are other indications that Fielding thought superior boys unlikely to be Andrewses and Partridges.

Partridge is a fine example of what in more recent times used to be known in middle class idiom as a little man, and he is treated by Tom as much as by the author with appropriate tolerance and condescension. An even subtler example is that of Sergeant

Atkinson in *Amelia*. Unlike Partridge he is raised after a time from his lowly social level when he receives a commission. Before that happens Amelia has an embarrassing moment when she thinks Mrs Ellison is going to marry him and talks to her about what a good idea it is. 'My marriage with a sergeant!,' exclaims Mrs Ellison, amazed that she should be thought 'capable of such condescension,' but afterwards, 'with an affected laugh, turned all into ridicule' (*Amelia*, I, pp. 289-291). At this point, Amelia would think it perfectly normal for Mrs Ellison to marry beneath her and give her husband her social advantages. Afterwards, when Atkinson has achieved something like it by marrying Mrs Bennet and then confesses to Amelia that she is really the girl he has always loved without hope, their dialogue is in terms of Joe and Madam, and although Amelia is left confused and excited by the experience, it is not only her virtue that has protected her from him. Atkinson has come some of the way up to his wife's level, but he does not sound like Amelia's equal. Although he could not be written off as a little man, he does not qualify as a gentleman either.

The point is not that Fielding wants all such subtle distinctions to be respected and honoured, but he knows about them and uses them and gives no sign that he thinks they should be abolished in the name of common humanity. *Amelia* is the most class-conscious of his books, in the sense that one detects the forerunner of a twentieth-century public-school tone of voice in all the main characters. He may deplore the sound, but this is the way the world that he knows about works, and he has given up pretending that the voice that counts for most in all conflicts is that of a cheerfully neutral foundling.

Fielding did not in fact leave us to work that out entirely for ourselves. In *Tom Jones*, he wrote about the different styles of conversation in low life and high life that in the one the historian 'will easily find examples of plainness, honesty and sincerity; in the other of refinement, elegance and liberality of spirit; which last quality I myself have scarce ever seen in men of low birth and education' (*Tom Jones*, II, p. 159). In other words, Fielding's egalitarianism is crossed with a belief in social determinants which has both a conscious and an intuitive side. Sometimes he manages to sound as if he thinks of himself as one of the very few living experts writing on the subject (the 'higher order of mortals' provide a 'sight to which no persons are admitted, without one or other of these qualifications, viz., either birth or fortune, or. what is equivalent to both, the honorable profession of a gamester' — *Tom Jones,* III, p. 93).

One does seem to get a better idea of Fielding by taking into account his black view of human nature and his class-consciousness. It also helps to recognize his susceptibility to female charms, which stands in some contrast to the exalted note he tends to strike on the subject of women. In the case of Fanny, who has little to say for herself, the charm is mostly physical: 'she was so plump that she seemed bursting through her tight stays, especially in the part which confined her swelling breasts' (*Joseph Andrews,* p. 175). Sophia' bosom we are meant to contemplate less familiarly, thinking rather of 'Nitor splendens Pario marmore purius,' a splendour purer than marble (*Tom Jones,* I, p. 148), but although not a loquacious person she behaves and talks on a few occasions in a distinctively feminine rather than, as we might have feared, a divine way. The parallel that could be established between her view that Tom is more to be censured for having talked loosely about her than for sleeping with other women, and Mrs Waters' indifference about his lack of devotion as long as she can have him for the night, might infuriate the heroine's admirers, and one would hasten to admit that these are parallel lines on different levels; but they suggest a similar feeling for female psychology on the part of the author.

The same impression is given by some of his observations about Amelia's rival, Miss Matthews. Her week of 'criminal conversation' with Booth in prison should count less against her, who has been in love with him for years, than against Booth himself. Unfairly, Fielding brings Booth out on top and turns viciously against poor Miss Matthews as soon as Amelia appears in the prison. Later on we meet her 'swearing bitterly' at the masquerade, and again uttering 'a most outrageous oath' when she forces Booth to have a meal with her (*Amelia,* II, pp. 195 and 280). The last we hear of her confirms our worst fears when it turns out in the final chapter that she grew very disagreeable and immensely fat afterwards. All this should not make us forget how touching she was in her devotion to Booth, considering every word he spoke a further proof of the marvel of his personality; nor that she paid for his release from prison without a moment's calculation. It looks as if

Fielding was divided on the subject of Miss Matthews' faults and merits in the early part of the novel — not perhaps doubting that she was reprehensible, but unable to prevent himself enjoying her excitement over Booth. In the end she has to be sacrificed for the sake of married happiness, but by that time her role in the book, unlike her figure, has grown so thin that our image of her is hardly affected. She remains the girl who, when Booth wanted to omit from his story a tender scene with Amelia, said that she would like him to repeat 'if possible, every syllable which was uttered on both sides,' and who assured him that for such a husband she would 'have leaped into the first fishing-boat I could have found, and bid defiance to the wind and waves' (*Amelia,* I, pp. 110 and 133).

Although withholding details of her physical attractions, Fielding in Miss Matthews gives us a further hint that his appreciation of women went beyond the pretty virtue of some of them. Nor would he expect us to expect anything different, judging by the story the narrator tells us at the end of Book I, ch. 6 of *Amelia,* in connexion with Miss Matthews. This concerns an innocent-looking girl at the theatre, of whom one lady said to another that it was a pity that such innocence should be exposed to such temptations. I overheard this, says the narrator, and I agreed about the girl's appearance, but 'I myself (remember critic, it was in my youth) had a few mornings before seen that very identical picture of all those engaging qualities in bed with a rake at a bagnio, smoking tobacco, drinking punch, talking obscenity, and swearing and cursing with all the impudence and impiety of the lowest and most abandoned trull of a soldier' (*Amelia,* I, p. 41).

This story can be made to serve reflections in two different ways. The first leads back to the subject of Fielding's appreciation of women. Even if one should not think that the narrator would insist on being taken seriously as a former connoisseur of brothel life, the very casualness of the reference suggests that he judges virtue in women from a background that most of his later critics would lack, or deny. We could not hope to find Thackeray, or Henry James, or any American critic writing a book dedicated to his wife, invoking their own experience of prostitution, however long ago. The theatre-and-brothel anecdote links Fieldings with the world of Restoration beaux, much as he may have disliked their successors in his own time, rather than with that of bourgeois virtue.

At the same time, more tenuously but firmly enough, the story leads on to the rigid state of social conditions in the world of Fielding's novels. Nobody of any note in them attains a position in society through his own efforts, if we except Jonathan Wild's achievements in crime. If the leading characters are all better off at the end than when they began this is strictly due to luck, which includes inheritance and patronage. In the case of Joseph Andrews we can await the solution of his employment problem, after his dismissal by Lady Booby, with a light heart because he did not have far to fall and will presumably be able to clamber back into the servant class; but his luck is better than that, and he shoots up into the snug middle-class world of the Wilsons. Tom Jones's case is more worrying because all seems lost when he is thrown out by Allworthy; but when after a passing phase of ambition to fight the Jacobite invader he arrives in London he only has a few weeks of plot to live through before he is restored to an improved version of his former position. The worst case is that of Booth, trapped in a social network far too harsh for his type, which needs a welfare state; his lack of opportunity feels oppressive, and remains so even after he too has been elevated by a stroke of luck.

Fielding's world is one in which people cannot move; they can only hope that they will be moved by circumstances. 'In some countries you can believe in the life of struggle,' a Pakistani called Masood said to V.S. Naipaul as reported in *Among the Believers*. 'You can believe there will be results. Here there is only luck. In this country you can only believe in luck.'[21] It sounds exactly like Booth's world; and like Fielding's, one might think. In fact it looks truer of the world that Fielding created than of the one he lived in, and it does so primarily because he himself was by no means so helplessly dependent on blind chance. His theatre, his newspapers, his novels, his legal training, the Universal Register Office: he was frequently trying things, and if in the end he needed patronage to get his appointment as Justice of the Peace in 1748, one must at least say that he had struggled to qualify for this piece of luck.

His characters had less sense of opportunity than he did, and one is led to think that this was because he wanted it so. People were not necessarily all good or all bad; they were more likely to be

21. V.S. Naipaul, *Among the Believers* (London, 1981), p. 183.

mixtures, as he argued on several occasions, but whatever they were they remained. Similarly, they might be in intermediate social positions, neither up nor down; and again, they stayed where they were, unless something entirely improbable liberated them for sake of the narrative.

The static condition of people's lives is in contrast to what we regard as normal in the twentieth century. 'In taking this essentially static view of human nature Fielding was following the time-hallowed Aristotelian view,' Ian Watt has said.[22] Nowadays, development is seen as the normal state of characters in novels, and in life outside the novel no degree of confinement in job and duties is thought to prevent liberation and self-realization. It could be argued that we are in the habit of deceiving ourselves about our liberty to get away from personal and social limitations; and that although Fielding exaggerated the rigidity of the system his characters lived under, what he was exaggerating was a partial truth.

This exaggeration should be taken into account when we appreciate his moral judgment. If people cannot change either themselves or their conditions, praise and blame are only encouragement and discouragement; any influence they have on society could only be to heighten the contrast. Not entirely, Fielding would have objected: a certain amount of affectation can be rubbed off people if they are made to feel sufficiently ridiculous. This objection must be allowed. Some minor improvement may be possible even in Fielding's philosophy; but in the main one can say that his view is a hard one. There is no serious hope of any change in his characters' lives; and their trapped condition is certainly not going to be softened by any compassion from him. Strongly though he may commend the compassion shown by Tom Jones towards an incompetent highwayman, and towards the Miller family, he does not indulge in anything comparable himself. The

22. Ian Watt, *The Rise of the Novel,* p. 312. If this makes Fielding sound old-fashioned and remote, cf. Bertrand Russell, in 1946 writing that Greek philosophers including Plato and Aristotle 'thought — originally on grounds derived from religion — that each thing or person had its or his proper sphere, to overstep which is "unjust" ' and that this conception 'is one which is still widely prevalent' (*History of Western Philosophy,* p. 194).

characters he condemns have no hope of understanding or of extenuating circumstances. There is no appeal.

Hardness is not in all circumstances an unattractive quality. It makes for clarity of judgment and resonance of contrast, and it provides relief for the modern reader after too many excuses for the bad and the unpleasant because they are supposed to be victims without responsibility for themselves. At the same time, it is not a side of Fielding that is much advertised, whether by himself or by his critics. It is only in his views on the proper treatment of criminals, as in his enquiry into the causes of crime written in 1751, that touches of severity are unmistakable. When the Duke of Newcastle in 1753 wanted action against the gangs of robbers in London, he asked Fielding, and the problem was solved in a couple of months by his new company of thief-takers.[23] Fielding has in recent years been regarded in such a favourable light that one has difficulty thinking of him as an advocate of hanging ('This I am confident may be asserted, that pardons have brought many more men to the gallows that they have saved from it').[24] But there it is, in his novels as much as in the enquiry: he believed that if you were dealing with a truly bad character it was best to rid the world of him, by hanging him, or if he were fictional, by boiling him in narrative oil in the final chapter.

iv

After the earlier insistence on the difference between the author's own personality and his various narrating *personae,* it would be absurd to try a piece together a real Fielding from the evidence of his books. Even if one adds to the elements of his personality that he was eager to put forward some others that become visible unintentionally, the picture of the man himself is bound to remain patchy. Nonetheless, with all its lacunae, the image of him has more sound and movement and invites more response than that of any of his creations.

He might be called a man of contradictions as long as this is not made to seem an unusual quality. Nobody is free from contra-

23. Cross, *The History of Henry Fielding,* II, p. 284.
24. *An Inquiry into the Causes of the Late Increase of Robbers, &c.,* W.E. Henley Edition Vol. XIII, p. 121.

dictions, and although some people succeed in glossing theirs over better than others, even they are unlikely to maintain an appearance of consistency when they let themselves go as much as Fielding did. He is firm in his conviction that people need to be told what is wrong and dishonest about their conduct, but he never persuades us that he believed such admonitions could improve anyone. A boisterous enjoyment of life dominates much of his work, and determines the surface of his reputation, but the impression of human existence as a miserable and scandalous condition does not suddenly emerge in *Amelia;* it announces itself at numerous points in his earlier writings. Not for a moment would he tolerate the idea that the upper classes produced a better sort of person than the lower; at the same time the distribution of charm and moral fibre in his work heavily favours those of good birth and education. He tended to create women whose beauty was supported by a soft but unbending moral perfection; yet he fails to hide an easy-going forgiveness of blemishes in his feminine characters which makes them look insidiously attractive. He insisted on the plain directness of his view of human nature, divested of the frills and illusions of traditional romance; but he allowed himself all sorts of narrative improbabilities, stylistic *tours de force* and quotations from the classics to keep up literary appearances.

And why not? It is not as if we hope to find in Fielding answers to our problems of conduct and judgment. We are better served with a share in the experience of somebody making his way through the confusion of his ideas, his prejudices and his instincts, and coming out with a pattern of at least partial coherence. That is something novels can do, although usually more of the experience is transmitted through the characters than in Fielding, and we are rarely so continuously aware of the narrator who had to do all that work for us.

While Fielding's narrator does not take part in the story, he belongs to the same reality as the characters whose adventures he relates. There is less invention in him, one could argue, but this establishes only a difference of degree: although we need no invention to live, we certainly do to produce a coherent description of ourselves. Also the incompleteness of the image we get of him is comparable to that of any novel character, in that both inevitably consist of a limited number of hints and suggestions which more or less effectively evoke a human being. One could daydream that if Fielding had lived two hundred years later he might have decided to make his narrator descend into the arena, and have produced an autobiographical novel. Before that could happen, not only would the novel form have had to become more familiar: the later Fielding had to be ready to reveal himself to the public more than the early one was. For someone so eager to be heard in his own voice he is remarkably reticent, and although it may be ascribed to accident that little personal information about him is available, the accident suits him.

As it stands it can still come as a surprise after all these years that he decided to write something like a novel at all. From his angle of approach, it must have seemed an awkwardly middle-class genre, fatuous in its traditional form of romance and falsely intimate, with tradition and vision replaced by convention and glimpses, in the way Richardson practised it. At the same time it was the obvious choice if one had the talent to entertain an audience and had for various reasons exhausted the possibilities of the theatre; if one urgently needed money; and if one was brimming over with views sometimes on public affairs and even more on morality and private conduct.

What he refused to do, in the first instance, was to let his standards be obscured in a twilight of feeling. Serious judgments on human affairs were not to be filtered through the mouths of servant-girls. The revulsion at *Pamela* and its popular success that Fielding expressed in *Shamela,* could be seen as an indictment of a *trahison des clercs.* Perhaps Richardson could not be properly described as a *clerc;* that only made it worse that he should be a successful author nonetheless. In the Augustan world there was a vital tradition of fear and disgust at the decadence of civilization for Fielding to call upon. His willingness to explore new territory was not to be taken as meaning that he had finally moved to Grub Street. He was going to be the man of two worlds: the conservative progressive, the innovator with classical credentials.

Even in this respect he was to be forced into further contradictions. Much as he believed in theory in the idea of putting types of human being in their places, it restricted him in practice. Although he had ample opportunity for literary fun and games and also for intelligent discourse, he could not give his characters enough individual life to make his readers share their experience, as they did with those of Richardson. He saw that Richardson had opened up a territory worth exploring, as both his attempts to bring about a *rapprochement* and the frequently noted parallels between *Clarissa* and *Amelia* show. At the same time he maintained his links with his own tradition. He kept up a clearly recognizable narrator's voice even when he suppressed the reserved spaces where his voice could be heard without the distraction of the story; he brought in a wide variety of characters, even though travel was abandoned and the English landscape became remote; and he allowed some of his characters to speak for themselves, even if unfortunately those who profited most from this liberty were secondary ones, not the hero and heroine.

Amelia did not go down too well, then or later, but it is a much more substantial book if one listens to Fielding sorting out his doubts and certainties than if one tries to read it as a story in its own right, for its events and characterization. The examples given to prove this point could be multiplied many times over, but should perhaps be finally reinforced in two ways in particular.

On the one hand it is necessary to bear in mind that if the narrator no longer reserves for himself the large enclosures of *Tom Jones,* he can do without them because he is perfectly prepared to let his own voice sound through his characters. When Booth treats Miss Matthews to a disquisition on upper and lower life there is nothing in his words to colour the pale image we have of him; what we hear is the author of *Joseph Andrews:*

> To confess the truth, I am afraid we often compliment what we call upper life, with too much injustice, at the expense of the lower. As it is no rare thing to see instances which degrade human nature in persons of the highest birth and education, so I apprehend that examples of what is really great and good have been sometimes found amongst those who wanted all such advantages (*Amelia,* I, p. 139).

In other places Booth acts as Fielding's pawn rather than as his mouthpiece, with much the same effect. When he tests an author he meets in the bailiff's house with probing questions on Lucan's poetry and place among the classics, he never sounds like Amelia's husband; he is just one half of a satire showing up a dunce:

> He asked him, therefore, what was his opinion of Lucan in general, and in what class of writers he ranked him?

The author stared a little at his question; and, after some hesitation answered, 'Certainly, sir, I think he is a fine writer and a very great poet.'

'I am very much of the same opinion,' cries Booth; 'but where do you class him — next to what poet do you place him?'

'Let me see,' cries the author; 'where do I class him? next to whom do I place him? Ay — why — why, pray, where do you yourself place him?' (*Amelia*, II, p. 87).

Such passages show us aspects of Fielding as clearly as when he is addressing us directly, or when he returns to a descriptive vein familiar from earlier years:

He was just entering upon his story when a noise was heard below which might be almost compared to what have been heard in Holland when the dykes have given way, and the ocean in an inundation breaks in upon the land (*Amelia*, II, p. 326).

Secondly, the dominance of the narrator's presence over that of the characters, which can be observed in isolated quotations, becomes even more apparent from an inspection of a sequence of scenes such as occurs in chapter II, *In which the history goes forward*, of Book IX. This opens with Booth returning from the bailiff's house and tenderly embracing Amelia; the narrator does not 'attempt to describe' the scene, but

I will observe, that a very few of these exquisite moments, of which the best minds only are capable, do in reality overbalance the longest enjoyments which can ever fall to the lot of the worst.

As part of the narrative, this is a poor substitute for a glimpse of true love, but it can be accepted happily as a glimpse of the Fielding we know. Perhaps the same could be claimed for the passage that follows, describing Booth's little son saying all the right things to Dr Harrison, to prove to us the excellence of Amelia's instruction. If this perfect child seems slightly embarrassing, Fielding makes up for it immediately afterwards when he describes Mrs Atkinson who is congratulated by the doctor on her marriage, as 'perhaps a little more confounded than she would have been had she married a colonel.'

The next part of the sequence concerns the arrival of Colonel James, introduced with a swift piece of circular reasoning followed by a familiar twist:

While our little company were enjoying that happiness which never fails to attend conversation where all present are pleased with each other, a visitant arrived who was, perhaps, not very welcome to any of them.[25]

The colonel holds his own nevertheless, helped by Dr Harrison who engages him in conversation,

For the doctor was not difficult of access; indeed, he held the strange reserve which is usually practised in this nation between people who are in any degree strangers to each other to be very unbecoming the Christian character.

The use of 'strange' cuts this sentence off from any chance of counting as a description of the doctor: one is primarily conscious of Fielding inserting his judgment on contemporary manners, just as one hears him two paragraphs later in the explanation of Colonel James's contented appearance in spite of his disappointment at not finding Amelia alone:

The great joy which he suddenly conveyed into his countenance at the unexpected sight of his friend is to be attributed to that noble art which is taught in those excellent schools called the several courts of Europe. By this, men are enabled to dress out their countenances as much at their own pleasure as they do their bodies, and to put on friendship with as much ease as they can a laced coat.

The anti-hypocritical rhetoric is not well-aimed, with its nonsensical implication that the colonel would show himself a better man if he pouted as soon as things did not go his way; but it passes as a familiar piece of the author's mind.

And then the characters surprise us by coming to life themselves in the next paragraphs when Booth misinterprets Amelia's unwillingness to accept a dinner invitation from the colonel. Not aware that James wants to seduce her, he thinks her reluctance is due to reservations about Mrs James; and:

Amelia, who had far other suspicions, and began to fear that her husband had discovered them, was highly pleased when she saw him taking a wrong scent. She gave, therefore, a little in to the deceit, and acknowledged the truth of what he had mentioned.

25. It is worth comparing this use of 'perhaps' with its 'brilliant' use, as C.J. Rawson has called it, elsewhere in *Amelia:* see below, p. 158.

The prose in which this little deception is described holds back somewhat to make room for the Booths to manifest themselves. It produces one of those satisfying moments when the narrative of *Amelia* carries its own meaning without a covering explanation from the author. The experience does not in fact last much more than a moment. Soon the narrator is out in front again, telling us that Amelia finds the deception most unpleasant, but:

> as she knew the characters, as well of her husband as of his friends, or rather enemy (both being often synonymous in the language of the world) she had the utmost reason to apprehend something very fatal might attend her husband's entertaining the same thought of James which filled and tormented her own breast.

The remark about friend and enemy often being synonyms restores the narrator firmly to the position he has held for most of the chapter, and holds for most of the book. That is the form *Amelia* takes: an author presenting his novel, with occasional openings for the characters themselves to be seen.

In other words, the character of Fielding's work can be said to have remained the same even if the mood has not, and the pleasure of his company is of the same order. A readiness to appreciate the last book on its own terms and its own merits probably comes more easily once the way has been prepared by a little depreciation of the earlier ones. As long as these do not change places with *Amelia,* and acquire a reputation of failure and unreadability in their turn, the action may be beneficial. Without getting to the point where the books should be enjoyed equally, one can say that each of them has moments when it looks better than the others, and that readers who look down on *Amelia* are likely to be wrong about all of them.

If one considers how Fielding was torn between the old literary taste and the modern instinct, and reflects on his struggle to establish his own terms, one might feel some compassion for him, regardless of whether he himself indulged in this feeling in his books. He looks such a friendly man, forced into such a precarious role between periods of history; and when one thinks of the viciousness of literary polemics of his time, and compares it to his gentle mocking of Colley Cibber and his unwillingness to be personal about most other people's faults, there is a passing temptation to see him as too well-meaning for this world. It passes because he clearly knew when to stop being friendly. He could stand up for himself firmly enough, even if he believed in good nature. Listening to his treatment of mankind in general and of sections of it like critics, lawyers and innkeepers in particular, one is bound to realize that although he may have been more vulnerable than some of his terrifying contemporaries, he had an ample measure of contempt in him to keep the enemy at bay. There was no need for him to bottle up the intimate arrogance that all human beings share but that is more strongly developed in those who set out to impress the world at large, particularly in those who intend to impose 'a new species of writing.'

Fortunately Fielding was able to make room for himself. A delightful man in some ways, with a loud voice distinctly heard even at a distance of more than two hundred years.

V FIELDING AND OTHERS

i

It would be no use claiming unique originality in looking upon Fielding's novels as personal documents rather than works of literature functioning independently of their creator. Anyone turning a few pages of one of these books will note the intrusiveness of the narrator as a typical characteristic, and it has been discussed by critics in a variety of ways. With so much insight already available, we can only shift familiar elements of critical appreciation into a different pattern, hoping that some new light will be let through.

If this practice leads, as it has done in the present case, to some depreciation of the objective qualities of the works and a stronger emphasis on their value as an involuntary portrait of the author, it is unlikely to meet with general approval. A suspicion might arise that having started by treating one novelist in this spirit one will go on try the same thing with others, and the possibility is hard to deny. The work magnifies the author, and the author limits the work: a commitment to either of these principles will find ample opportunity to exercise itself all through the history of literature. Fielding is not exceptional in making his authorial presence felt; he is only an extreme example, and not everybody has regarded the presence as the key to the significance. He has been described from several other angles which give the objective qualities of his work more prominence. One of these is their structure as praised by Coleridge; another has been their morality, ever since the discovery of his real self under the rakish character suggested by Murphy; their philosophy has been rephrased in objective terms, and their psychological insights have been singled out for critical attention.

All these elements are worth studying, but in the last instance one may still feel that they should find their proper place as aspects of the entertainer who is addressing us. The study of the rhetoric as a quality in its own right by John Preston and Wolfgang Iser has not affected this priority. 'The book is *about* judgment, and the understanding necessary for good judgment. That is where the moral sense is located, in the analysis and evaluation of diverse judgments' says Preston of *Tom Jones*.[1] It sounds promising, as long as we are not meant to understand that judgment is the book's only subject, but it leads on to the view that through Allworthy's 'high-minded failures [...] we gain some of our clearest impressions of the difficulty of judging well.'[2] It is impossible to imagine any reader having the experience suggested by these pronouncements. We would well advised to refrain from throwing stones at Mr Allworthy, but the difficulty of judging people is a tenser problem than his casual neglect of the available evidence can show. Preston presents his reader with a number of intellectual exercises which have a pleasing quality on their own, but it happens repeatedly that one is unable to interpret his subject in their terms. 'The author leaves the book to itself, or rather, to the reader. In other words, Fielding has been able, by means of the plot, to create a reader wise enough to create the book he reads.'[3] Surely not. By all means let us think of the reader as creating 'the book' he is reading, but it is not fair to imply that he would have been too lazy for this if he had not been forced by Fielding's rhetorical ingenuity.

The same idea that the reader is a passive recipient until Fielding persuades him to think for himself occurs in Wolfgang Iser. 'As the text invites him to imagine for himself what would be the right reaction to the given situation, he is bound to make the necessary adjustments consciously, and this process must in turn make him conscious of himself ...'[4] It is often a problem trying to decide who if anyone coincides with 'the reader' and the 'we' and the 'one' that critics send out as reconnaissance parties, but one usually ends up imagining at least a few people who might. The trouble with the Preston and Iser reader is that no one can be imagined who actually behaves as Fielding's rhetorical cunning is said to persuade or to force him to do. It is not Fielding who has created his

1. John Preston, *The Created Self*, p. 117.
2. ibid., p. 128.
3. ibid., p. 113.
4. Wolfgang Iser, The Implied Reader, p. 36.

reader: it is literary criticism, and like other literary figures the creation has no objective existence outside the pages of its authors. Either a reader judges for himself anyway, with or without invitation; or if he is of a sluggish disposition he will just use the book as a distraction from other forms of boredom, and resist without difficulty attempts to create him into shape of a critical moralist. 'We, not our texts, are the makers of the meanings we understand, a text being only an occasion for meaning':[5] and this is the way it always works.

Those who credit Fielding with secret weapons of literary technique achieve a similar result as those who admire all his human qualities: he grows to a size somewhat above the natural, like a statue of himself. On the whole the human qualities can be said to have been the major concern of a generation before the present one. Works like those of Cross and Blanchard are marked by an unwillingness to make any statement that could be construed as a slight on their hero; if they allow him weaknesses it is done mostly for the sweetness of forgiving him.[6] In the present age, with less need to defend the work or the man against detractors, judgments are more restrained. There is little of the policy of protection and praise for Fielding in all circumstances to be found in the works of J. Paul Hunter or Glenn W. Hatfield or Martin Battestin or C.J. Rawson.

What we get instead is structures of interpretation and association that once again suggest that the novelist must be a giant among human beings. The theories of Preston and Iser do this by crediting him with remote control over the inattentive reader's mind. Other critical views achieve it by sheer complexity of analysis and phrasing. When in *Jonathan Wild* Laetitia Snap is angry with Theodosia and Fielding makes her explain that she will never want to live in the same house again 'with the trollop, whom she detested so much the more because (which was perhaps true) she was her own sister,' the reader's chuckle is supported by C.J.Rawson in: 'That brilliant "perhaps" draws attention to what is implied to be a common but shocking "unnaturalness", which the narrator has, in the same breath, fully sized up. The under-

5. E.D. Hirsch, Jr., *The Aims of Interpretation*, p. 36.
6. Frederic T. Blanchard, *Fielding the Novelist* (1924), and Wilbur L. Cross, *The History of Henry Fielding* (1918); both passim.

stated brevity, in context, modulates without discomfort into and out of blowsy mimicries, and insisten rotundities of elaboration ...'[7]

Such a pronouncement lifts Fielding's swift little irony on to an academic plane where only trained intelligences can hope to capture its full meaning. At this level, criticism turns into an exercise which the reader should enjoy for its own sake rather than for its elucidation of the text it is concerned with. Most of us would as little think of using Rawson's interpretation to get a closer view of *Jonathan Wild* as we would J. Paul Hunter's to understand the interpolated stories of *Joseph Andrews* and *Tom Jones,* which he says 'ruthlessly contrast methods that ask and get simplistic or inverted responses different from those elicited by Fielding's own narrative method — a method more comprehensive, more tonally diverse and capable of reaching a range of responders, and so complex as to subsume within it demonstrations of bad rhetoric and its results.'[8]

A novelist who could do such things, most readers would be found to feel, is not within critical reach of the layman, who can only bow his head and accept his inadequacy. The best thing for the layman to do will be to return to the novels themselves, which look relaxingly accessible and comprehensible by the side of much of the criticism, even if they are two hundred years older. The Fielding he encounters there is an entertaining raconteur and a man of incisive intelligence and untiring energy, but normally human nevertheless, with his contradictions and misconceptions and his desire to please. There is a whole range of reactions that his writing provokes, from the closely involved to the distantly uninterested. One is hard put to believe that any reader could be constantly absorbed by him; it is equally difficult to imagine anyone being disgusted, or sent to sleep.

When Fielding fails to arouse our interest, this can sometimes be ascribed to the passage of time, which has removed some of the freshness from his handling of his subjects. On the other hand, the centuries may have compensated him somewhat by adding a historical curiosity value. A slight loss, on balance, has not made

7. Claude Rawson, *Henry Fielding and the Augustan Ideal under Stress*, p. 84.
8. J. Paul Hunter, *Occasional Form*, p. 156.

his position in relation to us essentially different from that of the modern novelist, whom we are just as unlikely to read in un-interrupted absorption. Anyone who has been privileged on occasion to meet novelists or just to observe them at close range knows that they are not consistently more probing and en-lightening in their utterance than many other people. Talent may make a difference once they start writing, but a limited one. The indispensable part of a novelist's talent is for using words and for narrating; it can operate happily in conjunction with an average insight into human motives and social relations. It is true that its possessor tends to look more controlled and commanding in writing than in talking, as his weaknesses of temper and intel-ligence and manners get overlaid by the firmness of his style. The sensible reader will not be overwhelmed by such hints of superiori-ty; he will be aware that the author even when writing is a person with a certain amount of invention and discovery to communicate, but not of course all the time. As Fielding himself wrote in 1740, in imperfect prose as if to strengthen the content with the form:

> ... no Narcissus hath hitherto discovered any mirror for the understanding, no knowledge of which is to be obtained but by the means Mr Locke prescribes, which as it requires arts and pains, or in other words, a very good understanding to execute, it generally happens that the superiority in it, is a cause tried on very dark and presumptive evidence, and a verdict commonly found by self love for ourselves.[9]

What the sceptical reader should nonetheless take into account is that the activity of writing may at times make the writer grow into a being superior to his usual self. Hours of concentration free from interruption or indifference may induce a state of heightened imaginativeness which brings insights normally beyond him. On the other hand these may fail to come, or flatter only to deceive, or remain tantalizingly just out of reach. The result is always in doubt, some of it perhaps better than it seemed while writing, some hopeless and some in between.

This is bound to be particularly true of novels, which as a rule are too long and complex to maintain a constant flow of imagina-

---

9. Champion no. 47, March 1 1740 (Henley Vol.XV, p.223), quoted in Ioan Williams, *The Criticism of Henry Fielding*, p. 78.

tive vitality, or for that matter to elicit it from the reader. Thinking about them as a genre one is not likely to overcome divided feelings. Sometimes their importance looks enormous, when one evokes their past and present and the intelligence that has gone into them and the memories readers have of their imaginary events and characters. At other times the mass of words seems more oppressive than stimulating, with all its tying-up of narrative loose ends, its characters looking too engaging to be true and its views so subtly divided between the character and the author and his implied double that one ever knows who thinks what.

ii

To some readers it may have looked as if part of the design of the earlier chapters was to reject an unusually large share of Fielding's stories and comments, leaving only bits and pieces to save the remnants of his reputation. Objections against such a practice could be raised even without a desire to defend Fielding. The whole of a novel should be appreciated as more than the sum of its details, and there is no need for all the parts to be separately vivid and all the insights to be universally true. They belong to the vision represented in that particular book, some essentially and some additionally; if they contribute to a whole that activates the reader's imagination, their appointed work is done, and any gem-like quality they may possess on their own comes as a bonus.

This is a sound argument except that it should not blur the distinction between priceless and negligible contributions. Our casualness about details needs to be kept within bounds. Admirers of authors run a risk of becoming as generous to them as lovers, wanting them to be wonderful and finding enchantment in their faults. It even looks as if there is a point on the scale of admiration beyond which books take on a quality of holiness: believers wonder what obscure parts of the text may mean without allowing for the likelihood that the obscurity may be due to tangles in the thinking or the writing.

The sanctification of literary works is a phenomenon familiar from relations between some modern writers and their admirers, where it is normally balanced by the rejection and vilification of other writers, or of the same ones by different readers. Literary judgment has a built-in extremist tendency which may come out at any moment and help devotees, at the cost of their sense of proportion, to feel that they belong somewhere in the intellectual spectrum. In its more moderate forms, an unwillingness to admit that brilliant minds spend much of their time plodding or relaxing instead of sparkling also confuses judgment. Doubtless it may be said that one of the pleasures of literature is that it invites us to concentrate the mind somewhat longer and more frequently than we normally do. Still, even when occupied with books our attention comes and goes, and while this phenomenon can in part be ascribed to our erratic quality as readers, it should be recognized that writers also normally produce uneven performances.

There are undisputed major authors whose works make this recognition fairly easy. Dickens may be as good an example as any; Thackeray is certainly one of them. On the other hand there are cases like that of Jane Austen who has a reputation of being near-flawless in her control over her carefully circumscribed subject-matter. Fielding's general reputation can probably be situated somewhere halfway between these extremes; but among supporters and specialists it stands much nearer to Jane Austen's.

In fact Jane Austen on closer inspection turns out to be as unreliable in judgment and imagination as anybody when her subjects gets out of hand, which perhaps happens to her less frequently than to most others. Kingsley Amis has pointed out for instance that *Mansfield Park,* while it may be the best of her novels, shows too much of 'the Austen habit of censoriousness where there ought to be indulgence, and indulgence where there ought to be censure,' and that Fanny Price, the heroine whose happiness we are meant to hope for, is 'a monster of complacency and pride.'[10] One could not agree more, and surely, although only a madman would ask for her to be relegated to a lower division of English literature, it is right to say that no clear estimate of her can be formed unless we allow her brilliance to be offset by her banality.

Even more revealing as a foil to Fielding may be the case of Henry James, who was such a conscientious craftsman that one might think he would have been horrified at the discovery of lifeless passages in his narrative, and have removed them at once; but they are still here. Perhaps he never noticed how frequently he put the

10. Kingsley Amis, *What Became of Jane Austen?* pp. 13-16.

communication with his reader in peril by writing too much. It is not only a matter of refining views of subjects from various angles; often it is one of repeating himself, in different words. 'I delight in a deep-breathing economy and an organic form,' he wrote in the Preface to *The Tragic Muse*;[11] but he is proudly wasteful at times.

The point could be illustrated with Chapter 42 of *The Portrait of a Lady*, the one that in the Preface to that novel James singled out for admiration ('It is obviously the best thing in the book'[12]), but more economically we can take the opening paragraph of Chapter 19, where the feelings of Isabel Archer about the early part of her friendship with Madame Merle are described. A little less than the first half of the paragraph would be just as enlightening as the whole of it is, or more so because our attention would not be confused by the impatience that begins to arise with 'The gates of the girl's confidence were opened wider than they had ever been,' when we have just been told that that she was more intimate with Madame Merle than she had been with anyone before. A few lines lower down we learn that there was no doubt that Madame Merle 'had great merits — she was charming, sympathetic, intelligent, cultivated. More than this (for it had not been Isabel's ill-fortune to go through life without meeting in her own sex several persons of whom no less could be fairly said), she was rare, superior, and pre-eminent. There are many amiable people in the world, and Madame Merle was far from being vulgarly good-natured and restlessly witty.' The parenthesis with its four negatives to complicate a simple positive statement looks like a caricature; the rest of those three sentences goes on about what we had heard earlier in the paragraph, and even within that short compass manages further repeats. It does not improve matters when James adds 'She knew how to think — an accomplishment rare in women,' because that is one of those cases where we cannot tell whose reflection we are hearing. Probably it is best interpreted as half-ascribed to Isabel, and completed by the author who makes her half-responsible for the preposterous implication that the world is used to men being good at thinking.

It is a fine specimen of a disastrous Jamesian paragraph, but there may be readers who admire it, considering perhaps that the

11. *The Art of the Novel* (New York, 1934), p. 84.
12. *The Portrait of a Lady* (Oxford, 1948), p. XVIII.

repeats give it the weight required at this point in the novel. More subtly, some might think it good and bad at the same time: good in that it gives us the authentic sound of the Master's voice, bad in that it depresses our imagination with excess verbiage. An ability to be simultaneously aware of the goodness and the badness of a passage is most useful quality in a novel reader, helping to overcome bafflement and loss of interest. It puts him on an equal footing with the writer beause that is how he himself lives, alternating between goodness and badness; and it gives his judgment full scope.

A reader can only make sense of a literary text if he possesses an imagination comparable to that of the person at the other end of the communication process. He may be inspired and banal in different ways and to a different degree, but he should not be a human being of a different order. While ordinary people produce memorable statements at the rate of one every few weeks, some great minds may average several daily; that still means that most of what great minds produce also belongs to the unremarkable side of life. Nothing is gained by pretending that anyone's talking or writing is an unfailing source of wonder and admiration, unless one should be helplessly in love with the sound of the voice or the style of writing. There are times when one is shocked into awareness, or shudders, or has one's eyes opened, or is swept along; there are many more other times when one experiences none of these sensations, but accepts that life goes on and so do talking and writing.

It is in this context that it seemed useful to subject Fielding to a treatment that may occasionally resemble a process of cutting down to size. Of course he should be cut down to size; it is precisely his size that we want to deal with. How necessary it is to point this out one never quite knows. Do we sanctify novelists, classical or modern or both; or does nobody pay the slightest attention to any of their views? Dauntless in the face of contradictions, we may do both at the same time. In any case there can be little harm in breaking off another piece from the romantic image of the artist as lawgiver. 'Art is not the key to the universe, as the Romantics had believed; it is merely a pair of spectacles'[13] — or

13. Gabriel Josipovici, *The World and the Book*, p. 192.

possibly not just spectacles but a pair of unfamiliar eyes made available for us to see through.

Seeing what another has seen or imagined will not be worth trying for us if that other lives in a world of different dimensions. Unless we expect art and wisdom to be poured out over us from a higher level, the writer must be a person as troubled and incomplete as ourselves, only more acutely so. And this was the point of bringing out his faults and failures.

iii

In conclusion, it seems worth producing an argument of a social nature for seeing works of fiction as personal documents. This is that it may stimulate readers' willingness to discuss them. Disappointingly little discussion of literature goes on in modern society even among people who are professionally concerned with the subject. In theory, fiction with its vast amount of descriptions of familiar situations in familiar terms could provoke ceaseless comments and judgments. It might be thought that readers would enjoy pointing out qualities and felicities of novels to each other in delight or disapproval; but this hardly ever happens. Except in very unusual company one never hears more than two or three adjectives used to recommend or dismiss a book.[14] If the author of a generally recommended novel imagined he was conveying anything in particular to his readers he was apparently mistaken; he has only left an indistinct impression of excellence with some

14. There is a lifelike dialogue about books in Harold Pinter's play *Betrayal* (London, 1978), where Robert who is a publisher discusses with his wife Emma a book she thinks good, and he says their friend Jerry thinks it good too, but he himself does not want to publish it, and she asks why.

ROBERT: Oh ... not much more to say on that subject, really, is there?
EMMA   What do you consider the subject to be?
ROBERT Betrayal.
EMMA   No, it isn't.
ROBERT Isn't it? What is it then?
EMMA   I haven't finished it. I'll let you know.
ROBERT Well, do let me know.
        Pause.
        Of course, I could be thinking of the wrong book.

people, although there will be others whose indistinct impression is of incompetence.

One explanation of the difficulty we have in lifting the subject out of this area of indistinctness is undoubtedly that there is too much of it. As a consequence, it is rare for two people to meet who have recently read the same book and have comparably extensive recollections of it. If they read it some months before, the likelihood is that only a few salient points will be remembered, too little to sustain any sort of conversation; the rest will be overlaid by newer impressions of books or other forms of entertainment. Only a mnemotechnician of genius will be able to recall the finer points and the sense of a novel read ten years or a hundred books ago. Anybody below his level would have to read a book at least twice to be able to talk about it a year later; and few people do this.

A fair comment on the scarcity of discussion, in other words, is that in the midst of plenty most readers have too little to talk about. Even those who have the required recollections at their fingertips, however, will often be reluctant to let themselves go, for a different reason: a fear of making fools of themselves. It is far from easy to decide how to judge a novel — by what standards, how strictly applied and how to be rated in relation to each other. Most amateurs would rather not try. Unless they have the heavy authority or the unabashed humility that disarms opposition, they will tend to confine themselves to saying they have enjoyed a certain novel but feel unable to decide whether it counts as literature. They may have liked the wrong thing, and want it to be understood that they defer to the experts and to judgments more cultured than their own.

They cannot hope to be told by any professionals how it is done. The standards used in modern literary criticism are not available for public dissemination. Critics are content to represent a mystery. Out of current ideas and opinions and some idiosyncrasies of their own, they manage to fashion a critical taste self-assured enough to command respect at least in writing. When it comes to talking, many of them appear as unwilling as any amateur to commit themselves to specific appreciations, knowing perhaps that their terminology is a sensitive apparatus and will seize up when casually used.

Even if a critical terminology should be automatically available, literary discussions might be difficult to keep going for a further reason which is simply that it is a struggle for anyone, however well-read and well-trained, to explain what he sees in such a complex thing as a novel. Some encouragement and pressure will be needed for most people to accept this hazardous assignment, and virtually the only places where these are consistently provided are the universities. It is in the Departments of English that literature is still talked about even in our easily distracted times, but it cannot be said that the light they shed spreads beyond their own walls and inspires an interest in literature in the world outside. It would be an oversimplification to say that literary discussion occurs only among scholars, and perhaps among humble escapists who tell each other the plot. Doubtless people who talk about novels exist in a variety of places, sometimes organized into clubs and groups and classes. All the same, the typical novel-reader is most credibly pictured as a lonely silent figure, living a puzzled life on the borderline between the physical and the fictional worlds and finding both intangible.

It could be suggested that the relations between those two worlds might improve if readers allowed themselves to think of novels as the product of the writer's imagination before trying to consider them as works of literature, governed by unknown rules. This does not mean that they would look for bits of autobiography in them, or would expect to find a ragbag of the author's experiences suitably disguised. Even when the evidence suggests that he has thought it all up, detail by detail, and the novel obviously gives nothing remotely like the reflection of his life, it cannot help giving us the reflection of his imagination. It is true that what one makes of him through his book is unlikely to look identical with what one would see in the flesh, but the figure in the flesh does not deserve to be regarded as more real. The knowledge we acquire of a person at work or at a party, or in a conversation or an embrace, does not permit us to draw a more substantial character-sketch than what we see in a piece of writing. They are different aspects, all partially revelatory of one particular life, and none of them ever complete enough to contain its entire potential. No amount of writing will result in a human being, but even a little of it will sometimes enable us to enter another person's mind.

It is impossible to determine what proportion of readers will find satisfaction in seeing literature primarily as a manifestion of curious authorial personalities. Certainly not everyone will, and those who want nothing to do with it could effectively claim that they are closer to the dominant spirit of modern criticism. Are people more interested in the strange shapes of human nature or in the properties of the work of art? No doubt they differ, but what deserves to be argued against those who want criticism to be a discipline with a theory is that literature looks remote and esoteric enough to many readers as it is, and that they might discover more in it if they overcame the fear of its otherness.

Extremism would be unfruitful, and it should be admitted that critics who judge a novel without any reference to the individual whose vision animates it are as rare as those who interpret the whole genre as nothing but personal documents. The continuing debate can only make sense if it concerns itself with emphasis rather than exclusiveness, and continues to take into account that Fielding's novels are an extreme case, being of an extremely authorial design. In addition, it should be realized that here as elsewhere practical objections prevent a strict application of principles. Only the most strong-minded reader can be expected to maintain an awareness of an author's individuality all through a novel. It is a demanding and time-consuming way of reading, and always at one's back one senses the presence of the shelves full of books that threaten to remain unopened. In the end the solution has to be found in a compromise between excellent principles and lowly routine, with the half-comforting thought that the multiple complexities of the world will never let themselves be interpreted without intuition and some luck.

Fielding, in any case, benefits from being treated as a character who wrote books rather than as a collective noun for the books themselves, and he can survive under a hail of doubts and reservations. One is tempted to pay him a farewell compliment, saying perhaps that he has been a friend and an inspiration all along, but this would be a formality. More in accordance with the view of him presented here one could say that it remains worth determining where in his work we agree with him and where we differ from him; where he is at his best, and where at his most characteristic. Taking him seriously in this sense, we will naturally preserve a detachment from his shining heroes and his wholesome philosophy. His great achievement is not the unlikely stories he has left us, nor the faint hopes for mankind that go with them. It is that after all these years we can still recognize an individual voice when he addresses us; that he makes it relatively easy to stay with him and read on through passages where he strikes a wrong note or touches no chord at all, and to accept that these form part of the price of exploring life in comfort through the medium of fiction.

Excellence, as was suggested in the Preface, is never a continuous phenomenon. Every reading experience is bound to combine insight and blankness, sympathy and estrangement, delight and boredom. If this study has managed to clarify the process for the reader of Fielding, it has done what it was meant to do.

SELECT BIBLIOGRAPHY

Fielding

The only complete edition of Fielding's works until the Wesleyan Edition is completed remains W.E. Henley's, in 16 vols., published in New York in 1903 and reissued in 1967.

For the sake of uniformity all page references have been made to that edition, except in the case of *Shamela* which is not included by Henley but accompanies Joseph Andrews in the Wesleyan Edition volume, edited by M.C.Battestin (Oxford, 1967).

The Wesleyan Edition also includes *Tom Jones,* edited by M.C. Battestin and F. Bowers, Oxford 1974; *Miscellanies,* Volume I, edited by H.K. Miller, Oxford 1972; and *The Jacobite's Journal and Related Writings,* edited by W.C. Coley, Oxford 1974.

Others

Addison, Joseph. *Essays on the Pleasures of the Imagination.* London, 1834.

Allen, B. Sprague. *Tides in English Taste (1619-1800).* 2 vols. Cambridge, Mass., 1937, repr. New York 1958.

Alter, Robert. *Fielding and the Nature of the Novel.* Cambridge, Mass., 1968.

Amis, Kingsley. *What Became of Jane Austen? and other questions.* London, 1970.

Battestin, Martin C. *The Moral Basis of Fielding's Art.* Middletown, Conn., 1959.

— — —.*The Providence of Wit.* Oxford, 1974.

Bentley, Eric. *The Life of the Drama.* London, 1965.

Bissell, Jr. Frederick Olds. *Fielding's Theory of the Novel.* New York, 1933.

Blanchard, Frederick T. *Fielding the Novelist.* New Haven, 1927.

Booth, Wayne C. *The Rhetoric of Fiction.* Chicago/London, 1961.

— — —. *The Rhetoric of Irony.* Chicago/London, 1974.

Brooks, Douglas. *Number and Pattern in the Eighteenth-century Novel.* London, 1973.

Carnochan, W.B. *Confinement and Flight.* Berkeley, 1977.

Collins, Anthony. *A Discourse concerning Ridicule and Irony.* London, 1729.

Coolidge, John S. 'Fielding and "Conservation of Character" ', *Mod. Phil.,* Vol. XVII no. 4 (1960), 245-259.

Coventry, Frances. *An Essay on the new Species of Writing founded by Mr. Fielding.* London, 1751.

Crane, R.S. 'The Concept of Plot and the Plot of *Tom Jones,*' R.S. Crane, ed., *Critics and Criticism Ancient and Modern.* Chicago, 1952.

Cross, Wilbur R. *The History of Henry Fielding.* 3 vols. New York, 1918.

Digeon, Aurélien. *Les Romans de Fielding.* Paris, 1923.

Donaldson, Ian. *The World Upside-down.* Oxford, 1970.

Donovan, Robert. *The Shaping Vision.* Ithaca, 1966.

Downey, James. *The Eighteenth-century Pulpit.* Oxford, 1969.

Ehrenpreis, Irvin. *Fielding: Tom Jones.* London, 1964.

Eliot, T.S. *Selected Essays 1917-1932.* London, 1932.

Ellis, John, M. *The Theory of Literary Criticism.* Berkeley/London, 1974.

Empson, William. 'Tom Jones,' *Kenyon Review,* no. 20 (1958); repr. in *Henry Fielding, A Critical Anthology* (see under C.J. Rawson).

Fielding, Sarah. *The Adventures of David Simple.* London, 1744. (O.U.P. ed., London 1969).

Frey, Bernhard. *Shaftesbury und Henry Fielding.* Bern, 1952.

Fussell, Paul. *The Rhetorical World of Augustan Humanism.* Oxford, 1965.

George, M. Dorothy. *Hogarth to Cruikshank.* London, 1967.

Harrison, Bernard. *Henry Fielding's Tom Jones.* London, 1975.

Hassall, Anthony J. 'Fielding's Amelia'. *Novel,* Vol. V. no. 3 (1971), 225-233.

Hatfield, Glenn W. *Henry Fielding and the Language of Irony.* Chicago, 1960.

Heiserman, Arthur. *The Novel before the Novel.* Chicago, 1977.

Highet, Gilbert. *The Classical Tradition.* Oxford, 1947.

Hirsch, Jr., E.D. *The Aims of Interpretation.* Chicago, 1976.

Homes, F. Dudden. *Henry Fielding, his Life, Works and Times.* Oxford, 1952.

Humphreys, A.R. *The Augustan World.* London, 1954.

Hunter, J. Paul, *Occasional Form.* Baltimore/London, 1975.

Hutchens, Eleanor Newman. *Irony in Tom Jones.* Alabama, 1965.

Hutcheson, Frances. *An Inquiry concerning Beauty, Order, Harmony, Design* (1725), ed. by Peter King. The Hague, 1973.

Iser, Wolfgang. *Henry Fielding und der Englische Roman des 18. Jahrhunderts.* Darmstadt, 1972.

— — —. *The Implied Reader.* Baltimore/London, 1974.

James, Henry. *Selected Literary Criticism.* Ed. by Morris Shapiro. London, 1963.

Jarrett, Derek. *England in the Age of Hogarth.* London, 1974.

Johnson, Maurice. *Fielding's Art of Fiction.* Philadelphia, 1961.

Josipovici, Gabriel. *The World and the Book.* London, 1971.

Karl, Frederick A. *The Development of the English Novel in the Eighteenth Century.* London, 1975.

Knox, Norman. *The Word Irony and its Context, 1500-1755.* Durham, N.C., 1961.

Leavis, F.R. *The Great Tradition.* London, 1948.

Levine, George R. *Henry Fielding and the Dry Mock.* The Hague, 1967.

Loftis, John. *The Politics of Drama in Augustan England.* Oxford, 1963.

May, Georges. *Le Dilemme du Roman au XVIIIe Siècle.* Paris, 1963.

McBurney, William H. *Four before Richardson.* Lincoln/London, 1967.

McKee, John B. *Literary Irony and the Literary Audience.* Amsterdam, 1974.

Miller, H.K. *Essays on Fielding's Miscellanies: A Commentary on Volume One.* Princeton, 1961.

Moore, Cecil A. *Backgrounds of English Literature.* Minneapolis, 1948.

Muecke, D.C. *The Compass of Irony.* London, 1969.

Myers, O.M., ed. *The Coverley Papers,* from the Spectator. Oxford, 1908.

Palmer, Eustace. '*Amelia,* the Decline of Fielding's Art,' *Essays in Criticism,* Vol. XXI, no. 1 (1971), 135-151.

Paulson, Ronald. *Satire and the Novel in Eighteenth-century England.* New Haven/London, 1967.

— — —. *Hogarth, his Life and Times.* 2 vols. New Haven/London 1971.

Preston, John. *The Created Self.* London, 1970.

— — —. 'Is there a Good Book on Fielding?', *Essays in Criticism,* Vol. XXI, no. 1 (1971), 91-100.

Price, Martin. *To the Palace of Wisdom.* New York, 1964.

Rawson, C.J. *Henry Fielding and the Augustan Ideal under Stress.* London, 1972.

— — —, ed. *Henry Fielding, a Critical Anthology.* Harmondsworth, 1973.

Richetti, John J. *Popular Fiction before Richardson.* Oxford, 1969.

Robert, Marthe. *Roman des Origines et Origines du Roman.* Paris, 1972.

Rogers, Pat. *Grub Street.* London, 1972.

— — —. *The Augustan Vision.* London, 1974.

— — —. *Henry Fielding.* London, 1979.

Sacks, Sheldon. *Fiction and the Shape of Belief.* Berkeley/London, 1964.

Sakuma, Makoto. *Laughter as a Weapon.* Tokyo, 1974.

Shesgreen, Sean. *Literary Portraits in the Novels of Henry Fielding.* De Kalb, Ill., 1972.

Spearman, Diana. *The Novel and Society.* London, 1966.

Tave, Stuart M. *The Amiable Humorist.* Chicago, 1960.

Thackeray, William Makepeace. *The English Humourists of the Eighteenth Century.* London, 1853.

Tillyard, E.W.M. *The Epic Strain in the English Novel.* London, 1958.

Van Ghent, Dorothy. *The English Novel.* New York, 1953.

Voogd, P.J. de. *Henry Fielding and William Hogarth, the Correspondence of the Arts.* Amsterdam, 1981.

Ward, Ned. *The London Spy* (1703), ed. by Arthur L. Hayward. London, 1927.

Watt, Ian. 'The Ironic Tradition in Augustan Prose, ' *Restoration and Augustan Prose,* papers by R. Sutherland and Ian Watt. Berkeley, 1956.

— — —. *The Rise of the Novel.* London, 1957.

West, Rebecca. *The Court and the Castle.* London, 1958.

Willey, Basil. *The Eighteenth-Century Background.* London, 1940.

— — —. *The English Moralists.* London, 1964.

Williams, Ioan, ed. *The Criticism of Henry Fielding.* London, 1970.

— — —. *The Idea of the Novel in Europe, 1600-1800.* London, 1979.

Williams, Muriel Brittain. *Marriage: Fielding's Mirror of Morality.* Alabama, 1973.

Wright, Andrew. *Henry Fielding, Mask and Feast.* London, 1968.

INDEX

Curriculum vitae

John James Peereboom, geboren in Londen op 14 november 1924, doorliep in Haarlem een sindsdien opgeheven lagere school en het Stedelijk Gymnasium, waar hij in 1943 eindexamen deed. In 1945 ging hij Geschiedenis studeren in Leiden; in 1950 legde hij het doctoraal examen af. Na enige aarzeling en een periode als bureauredacteur bij de Nieuwe Rotterdamse Courant vertrok hij in 1953 naar Parijs; vier-en-een-half jaar leefde hij daar van free lance journalistiek voornamelijk over literatuur en theater. Van 1958 tot 1971 deed hij voor NRC, Parool en op het laatst NRC-Handelsblad hetzelfde soort werk in Londen, aangevuld met televisiejournalistiek meestal voor de NCRV. In 1971 werd hij wetenschappelijk medewerker aan de Universiteit van Amsterdam, om het moderne drama dat hij in Londen bestudeerd had en later ook andere literatuur te doceren. Hij schrijft nog steeds recencies voor NRC-Handelsblad, draagt bij aan verschillende tijdschriften zoals Hollands Maandblad, Maatstaf en de Dutch Quarterly Review, en heeft een kleine literaire productie op zijn naam waarvan een deel in twee bundels, *Ik ben niets veranderd* en *De gravin van Loosdrecht,* is uitgekomen bij de Arbeiderspers.